The American State of Canaan

Alfred de Grazia

THE AMERICAN STATE OF CANAAN

The Peaceful, Prosperous Juncture of
Israel and Palestine as the 51th State of the
United States of America

METRON PUBLICATIONS

Published by
METRON PUBLICATIONS
P.O. Box 1205
PRINCETON NJ 08542-1205
ISBN#978-60377-076-7
Library of Congress Catalog Number : 200894526
Copyright © 2008 by Alfred de Grazia

« *What risks attend making oneself the Leader in counseling a Thing, and the more ot has of the extraordinary, the greater the risk one runs.* »
Machiavelli, *Discourses*

Dedicated to
The Builders of the 51st State

TABLE OF CONTENTS

A CANAAN STATE BRINGS MIDEAST PEACE

Israel is a deeply troubled country, which is causing deep trouble wherever it turns. Palestine, its neighbor, is the most obvious of disastrously affected lands. America is despairingly engaged with both countries, although its true interest is invested in Israel. Strangely this interest is almost purely ideological -- psychological and sentimental, not at all in the usual export trade and investment, competing for power or in sports, or sending tourists, which explain international relations. And, for this intense sentiment it pays an enormous price. In fact all three countries pay a relatively gross price, both to one another and to the numerous countries that are drawn into the relationship, who also pay heavily, the whole of the Near East, that is, but more: the whole world!

I have been giving my late years to worrying about the situation, as if I were running the show, instead of being an 89-year-old helpless observer, devoid of means. You, my reader, and I both recognize that conditions there have been going from bad to worse, for years, now. And we know that no solution has yet occurred to bring peace and well-being to the region. But recently I reached out and I imagined a solution. It is too early to say. Still, I can bring it forth.

I asked myself a new sort of question: Why should we not demand that the intertwined countries of Israel and Palestine become a single State of the United States? What a shocking idea it was at first! Yet, day by day, its possibilities accumulated into probabilities. In the end I decided that not only was it a probable solution, but maybe the only solution, and I better bring it forth, as not only my time is running out. I addressed its challenges one after another. Soon I put aside other work and got into writing a book in pursuit of the idea, and now the book is finished and here it is: *The American State of Canaan,* the 51st State of the Union, suited to and fit for the vastly important task of bringing peace and welfare to the Near East, the United States, and ultimately the World.

❖ ❖ ❖ ❖

A CANAAN STATE BRINGS PEACE

Canaan would encompass and unify the territories presently constituting Israel and Palestine. Palestine would instantly rise up from its low place both in world regard and in well-being. And Israel would be no longer uniquely irresponsible, incorrigibly law-breaking, and threatening global disaster. And America would be safer, stronger, richer, friendlier – a good neighbor to the world.

We urge that Israel and Palestine should make joint application for Statehood to Congress, and that it be admitted to the Union as soon as possible. Time is indeed running out. No one doubts the threat to the countries concerned, to the region, and to the world. Alone or interacting, Israel, the USA, Russia, France, China, Britain, India and Pakistan could heavily damage civilization, wipe out most of mankind, and do so quicker than the Global Warming that is coming upon us.

The United States is presently composed of 50 States, united under a Constitution over 200 years old that was originally agreed to by special popular conventions held in the States of the preceding Confederation. It was to go into effect when nine States approved it. And so it happened, after vigorous debate around the country. A full thirteen States finally joined in.

THE AMERICAN STATE OF CANAAN

The Constitution has been amended infrequently; amendment is a cumbersome process. However, it needs be borne in mind that, from a behavioral point of view, the Constitution has really changed often and is in a condition of continual change. Within limits which themselves vary, the Constitution changes by usage, by the force of circumstances, by slightly different renderings by the Executive, Legislative and Judicial branches of the government, which are dutifully followed by everyone concerned with, or forming part of, the governments of the States and localities and the central Federation government in Washington, and wherever decisions are made in the ramified republic as it operates domestically and abroad.

Fortunately, an Amendment is not required in order to add a State to the Union. The last States to be admitted to the Union were Hawaii and Alaska, both in 1959. At present, the Island Commonwealth of Puerto Rico is the outstanding candidate to become the 51st State. It was a Territory at first. Then, to add some prestige, it was designated a Commonwealth. Its Constitution dates from 1952. Its languages are English and Spanish. Its citizens are American citizens and they elect a Governor, a Legislature and a Resident Commissioner who represents the Island in the House of Representatives, while voting only on Committee matters.

Recently its voters decided not to seek admission to the Union, at least not for the time being. They have a deal whereby they pay no national income tax on earnings on the Island. They also have two million Puerto Ricans who dwell on the mainland, with all rights, and these people, through their federal representatives, can lobby on behalf of the Island's wants. It resembles the Israelis' situation, whose American Jewish connections seem to give them all that they need in the way of representation, if not more.

Israel is a so-called sovereign state in a world of nearly 200 nation-states. Most of them are poor, underdeveloped, and with only a modicum of influence abroad. Israel declared itself a nation-state in 1948, complete with a Declaration of Independence, rather like that of the United States of 1776, but it has never been able to come to terms with a Constitution. What repeatedly broke up efforts to compose one was a deadlock between intransigent orthodox Jews and equally adamant secularists.

So it gets along with a group of basic laws, differing in importance, and pronounced and interpreted by the Judicial Branch of the Government, which is not always reliable. An erratic Executive Branch, subtending from a disorderly, multi-party Knesset or Parliament, can involve themselves in interpreting basic law rather more than is the case in America or France or England. The system lends itself to brokerage, changes of mind, and finagling.

Palestine, usually termed the Palestine Authority, has existed as a kind of government as long as contemporary Israel. However, as all the world knows, it is a cripple, suffering from continuous civil disorder, and has been repeatedly denied by a determined Israel and a pusillanimous world community the authority and powers needed to cohere and pretend to sovereignty.

The interacting duo are the core of what is arguably the world's most troubled region. Enormous effort and costs have gone vainly into stabilizing the pair of governments. For sixty-three years, their situation has been desperate. Both Israel and Palestine have taken a step backward for every step forward toward a bare peace – never mind all the other features that should go into ruling civilized peoples in this day and age.

❖ ❖ ❖ ❖

The two peoples have existed under trying conditions, but let me remind you what incompatible, sinister, incompetent, exasperating elements pervade, and periodically operate both of these governments, and why therefore the

14

transformation of the situation that is so discouraging into a tolerable polity absolutely requires the solution being proposed in this book – namely an arrangement whereby Israel-Palestine – these two aggregates – should be combined and enter the Union of the United States of America in equality with other States, as Canaan, the Fifty-first State.

In their internal affairs, in relations with each other, and in interaction with the world community and the United States itself, the two governments are dominated by just those elements that one would recruit to assure there would never be peace, prosperity, and progress. That is, the elite, those who have the most of what exists of power and goods – the rulers, from the top down to whatever lower echelons are given power to interfere with and dominate the behavior of others – includes an excess of unsavory elements. We speak of the elites both of Israel, with its incomparable superiority of means, and of Palestine, which exists in a poor way, deprived of most civilized tools for building a commonwealth. Nor is the USA elite far behind (or ahead).

We notice such rogues especially among security agents and police. We see them infiltrating the military, and remark how many politicians and officeholders are unstable desperados. They propel unruly gangs and crowds. They are profiteers in an arena teeming with fat contracts, subsidies, payoffs and various types of bribery. They connect up with international criminals (drug trafficking, money laundering, industrial and securities fraud, media manipulation, and insolent breakers of international law). False patriots (chauvinists) and traitors to humanity abound. If the leading elements of Palestine and Israel, and their American counterparts, were examined, rated, counted, they would show a high average score of malfeasance. The outcome of their dominating role is perforce the deplorable conditions that exist.

I do not claim that all of the elites are bad, nor that all who must and will come in to replace them will be good. I do claim that the difference between the governing groups before and after the achievement of Statehood will be more than sufficient to bring needed conditions of peace, stability, and progress to the two peoples. This one factor, this one change, occurring almost like the force of nature, will justify the new State. I estimate that an elite change of 20% will suffice, and that a larger change might well take place within several years of Statehood.

More will happen. Preferable trustees for a well-governed society, who are discouraged presently in Palestine and Israel, and among those Americans who might wish to cultivate an involvement with Israel, will come forward under the changed conditions of Statehood: teachers, moderate religious sectarians, students, legitimate businessmen, scientists, and generally an intelligentsia that offers balance, richness, and satisfaction to the inhabitants of a State.

Gathering Israel and Palestine into the United States of America as Canaan, its 51st State, will solve the crisis of the Middle East, and help make the world a habitable, just community. I say so as a political scientist and world citizen.

I am happy personally, for I would foresee an end to the Palestinian Nakba and a new better life for them coming out of my reflections. I have also fulfilled a duty to the many Jewish loves, relatives, friends, colleagues and ordinary Jews met with during my long life. The privilege of tying up a scientific obligation with human bonds is rarely possible, and, until recently, inconceivable even to myself, the author, under the circumstances. I feel now that, before 5 years have passed, Canaan can have become a fully functioning State.

Some days after the tragedy of September 11, over a million Jews and friends paraded down the avenues of New York City, carrying many banners, one proclaiming "America is Israel," and another: "Israel is America." The demonstration showed the great sorrow of Americans. It showed, too, a peculiarly intense connection that Jews felt to the disasters of September 11, a sense of being

17

embroiled in the chaos in which the 9/11 Event occurred. The attack was anti-Semitic as well as anti-American.

There are actually for the first time in 2,700 years the means to tell a generally true history of Canaan, carrying Israel and Palestine with it, and especially doing an acceptable job on the story of the past 63 years. Rewrite Hebrew history throughout the length of time of Judaism, but especially of the past 60 years of Israel. Uri Avnery has done a commendable brief account of the new Jewish history on the web. We disagree in that he believes that much more of the Bible is myth than do I. In my book on *The Iron Age of Mars,* I say that the early phrases of Hebrew tribalism took place in the hills of Western Arabia and only much later, when the Late Bronze Age came crashing down, did the Hebrews move up North via Babylon. So, as Kamal Salibi has shown, much of the Bible proves itself by correlating with place-names, locations and events of Western Arabia. (The clincher is Salibi's demonstration of the alternative vantage points of "Mt. Nebo" from which Moses is said to have looked down upon the Promised Land stretching West to the Sea - the impossible view from the Northern accepted promontory (al Siyagagh), the really possible view from el Nabawah, far to the South in Arabia.)

A CANAAN STATE BRINGS PEACE

We ought to correct the biographies of a number of Israeli (and American) leaders, such as Ben-Gurion, Rabin, Perez and Sharon, and also Harry Truman, Lyndon B. Johnson, George W Bush *et al.*, showing their attitudes in a true light and promote the biographies of leading Jews (and gentiles) who have earned the respect of humanity, like Hannah Arendt, Martin Buber, Albert Einstein, Uri Avnery and great intellectuals and artists such as Daniel Barenboim. And, I repeat, the brave scholars whom I will be calling on in the course of this work.

We should be teaching at all levels of civic education, formal and informal, in the classroom and on the streets, the evil nature of racism and the duties of truly democratic citizenship. We should teach the distinction between a strong pacifism and an erratic, rough militarism.

In Israel, among the Jews, the struggle is between the intelligentsia and the military garrison. In absolute numbers the two groupings are about equal. While the one works with humanist persuasion, by propaganda, by technological controls and by diplomacy, the militants are proponents of force, a tricky *Machtpolitik*. But since the military must elaborate a propaganda, and employ high technology, both in Israel and the USA, the military has been engorging the intelligentsia and the resources needed for peace and war in many areas of scientific research.

I think of the 60th Anniversary of the Declaration of the Founding of the State of Israel, which has been recently celebrated. Every effort has been made to exhibit and pretend to a Grand Success. Heads of state are dashing in and out of the country. Parades, cultural events, reams of self-congratulation spread everywhere. Military force and a remarkable technology are the principal exhibits in fact. Dare I ask: is it true? – Perhaps eight million Palestinians would cry about it, so, too, millions of Lebanese and people of several other lands. And would not several million Israelis themselves prefer to celebrate elsewhere and for different reasons, other than the official reasons being trumpeted? But those Jews, who are the world's greatest magicians and entertainers, will produce a grand Roman triumph, with a resounding hurrah from the naive and deluded.

These have been a dreadful 60 years of Israel: not a day but that half its people were discontented and suffering disenchantment. A mind-searing, materially destructive, psychologically sickening, shameful struggle has been going on now for 60 years in the region of Palestine and carrying all around into the Middle East, into six countries, with more years to come. Is it not a disgrace to the leaders of Europe, the

Arab nations, the world's Jews and the United States of America, this struggle?

The costs can be figured in many ways. Beginning with frightful though mostly quick deaths, moving through physical wounds of all degrees of damage, psychic wounds from stony catatonism to lifetime PTSD, from interminable worry to frightful dreams of traumatized children who will become traumatized adults, and so forth.

But should we not include Palestine in the celebration of Israel? And are Lebanon's and Iraq's defeats to be celebrated as well? I fear so in all three cases.

A Marine general of the futile Vietnamese War, over which Israelis ought to ponder, when he was told: "We must win the hearts and minds of the Vietnamese people," retorted: "No, Sir. Grab them by the balls and their hearts and minds will follow!" This Vietnamese War was lost, first by the French, then by the Americans.

Sixty years and more have passed since WWII put an end to the worst splurge of human devaluation in history. But in sad part, it has continued. In the Near East, these 63 years have brought boundless pain and suffering, with a million terminated lives, ten million injuries, 500 million traumatic disorders, property destruction equal to all the material worth of Switzerland, and trillions of dollars cast to wild winds.

Several Israeli and Palestinian groups exist that might cooperatively propose and agitate in every way possible for Statehood. If the appropriate groups do not respond favorably to the urging of some of their members, then these members, with or without resigning from their groups, can form a new group on behalf of Statehood. In any event, the guiding group should be composed both of Israelis and Palestinians.

The "51st State" membership should expand and develop its program with maximum variety and energy not only in the USA and Israel-Palestine but in the Arab Refugee Camps and in as many countries as possible. After all, if the neo-Zionists neurotically insist on the worldwide presence of a "Jewish problem," the solution of the problem should be agitated wherever it exists.

The Canaan Movement should as soon as possible seek out legislative representatives who will introduce the proper Statehood Resolution, as I shall explain. Let me only stress, before concluding, that the American people – and upon them, including American Jews, all depends – have a proper set of attitudes to carry through to Canaan.

Public opinion surveys show the American people in a different light than is cast upon them by their politicians. A very strong majority supports American engagement in world affairs, rejecting isolationism. They fear the US role is getting unstable, however. They are not gung-ho on our being the only policeman and superpower.

A solid majority approves multi-lateral approaches to world problems and working through international institutions like the UN, and would give them more powers. People believe that US and global interests are compatible and they are worried about a number of social and environmental problems.

Still a plurality feels that the USA is doing more than its share. They hold contradictory views: that we spend unjustifiably more on international programs than on domestic ones (not realizing the actual sums spent) and when asked to set the preferred level themselves, they set it higher than the actual level.

Large majorities feel that the world likes us less and less, and are afraid of US force that will hurt them. This makes them want both more national security activity and doing less harm to other countries. They are in favor of selling democracy abroad, but without the use of force. They do not expect every country to take our salesmanship to heart, but they do want to apply pressure for freedom and human rights around the world. Most (69% in one survey, for instance) believe that the United Nations is the best means of promoting world democracy. But still a quarter of them think that the US can act more decisively and effectively alone.

Human rights are important enough, says a large majority in one survey, to give up a military base or lose a government's friendliness in defense of human rights. The people (though not the interest groups with which they may be implicated) do not mind the targeted country discriminating against us when we work to make them respect human rights.

Numerous polls show American majorities feeling that their country has a moral obligation to intervene to prevent a genocide. 69% in a Pew poll agree that "the US and other Western powers have a moral obligation to use military force if necessary to prevent one group of people from committing genocide against another."

The Israel government risks by its "slow genocide" of Palestinians to be switched over at any time to a most dreadful American public view that it is actually genocidal. Should that ever occur, US-Israeli symbiotics will collapse like a house of cards.

Other beliefs play into this operation, filling out the set of beliefs that make the Israeli position far less firm than it appears to be. For example, 85% of Americans assert that other countries should not be allowed to spend money to try to influence US elections. Israel and its American cohorts are in danger here, too, for there is a network of tactics whereby Israel helps its "friends" in high places in the US.

And in another survey, only 16% said the US "should not worry about what others think, but just think in terms of what is best for the US, because the world is a rough place." To the contrary, 79% thought the "good neighbors" policy is "ultimately in the best interest of the United States."

It is fair to say, I think, that most Americans *mean well*. But like us all, Americans must be inspired to *do well!*

CANAAN STATE, USA

A proposed State must have a name. Some people might feel bruised by a State named "Israel" or "Palestine." Others would feel a surge of exclusive patriotism. We see little chance of either name sufficing, and less chance of the awkward and forbidding name, "Israel-Palestine." I doubt that Joel Kovel's coinage would pass muster: "Palesrael."

So we make a bold suggestion. Most of us might prefer the smoother, more accommodating, and even historically more accurate name of "Canaan", as in New Canaan, Connecticut, USA, founded in early colonial times when the Bible had to be read by all. Puritan colonists were often convinced that they were reestablishing Israel. To these assiduous Biblicists, Jerusalem was out of reach, but a new Jerusalem would do fine.

I would also suggest that the name be pronounced *"cane'-an."* The name is easily spelled by my countrymen, most of whom cannot spell or pronounce States such as Arkansas, Massachusetts, Illinois, and Connecticut. (An astonishing 90% of Americans between the ages of 16 and 25 cannot find Israel on the outline map provided them by the National Geographical Society, and 50% cannot locate the USA!)

The citizens of Canaan can be called by the same word, "Canaans." We note that "Israelites" is no longer used for citizens of Israel, though correct for ancient Hebrews, and "Israelis" is used instead.

/ Until lately, the Bible has had everyone believing that the "Canaans" were the original inhabitants of inner Palestine, with the Philistines settled along the coast of the Mediterranean. When Joshua led the tribes of Israel into Canaan, legend has it that he did as he was told to do by Yahweh, by Moses (who had meanwhile died) and by the rabbis, that is: slaughter the Canaanites and any other group which he could subject to ethnic purging. (I prefer this term to "ethnic cleansing," which is euphemistic and unsuited to such a terrible process.)

This "Promised Land" (word of Yahweh) was to become a sacred region. The "Holy Land," got its appellation only a few hundred years ago, and is ultimately a Holy Land to hordes of true believers around the world, whose God-Hero, Jesus, held forth and was crucified there, or whose leader Mohammed let the term stand and recommended it to his myriads of followers.

But now foremost scholars in Israel, Germany, America, Britain, Denmark, and elsewhere tell us that the Hebrews were modest, backward "hillbillies," most likely Canaans themselves, but socially inferior to the Canaans of the lowlands. Just as, a century ago, the "hillbillies" of Kentucky, USA, and soon afterwards the Southern Blacks, moved up to Detroit to work in the booming automobile factories, the Hebrews moved down from their highlands to where jobs could be had and life was richer and more amusing. Nor did they kill off the Canaanites to take their land, whatever the Bible says in one of its several genocidal passages. Rather the Hebrews may have worked their fields and merged with them over time and in the course of natural disasters and wars. This follows the research and discoveries of archaeologist Israel Finkelstein, of the University of Tel-Aviv, and an international coterie of scholars, including several termed the "Copenhagen School..."

Thus, the latest research possessing scientific integrity places both Hebrews and Palestinians originally among the Canaanites, a large regional demographic grouping clustering along the banks and valley of the Great Jordan fracture, from North of modern Lebanon down to where it meets with Western Arabia and the head of the Red Sea.

Still, this is not the radical revision to end all radical revisions of the Bible stories. It is mainly the theory of the Tel Aviv archaeologists. To their North, at the American University of Beirut in Lebanon, there has been Professor Kamal Salibi, a Druse and a Christian. He places the original home of the Canaans along the Western Coast and hills of Arabia, Hebrews above and Canaanites below. It is from there that they pushed northwards, the Hebrews in parallel with the Canaanites, until they came to geographic Palestine, confining the Philistines and Phoenicians to the coastal regions.

The idea of the name Canaan came while doing research on my book, *The Iron Age of Mars,* where I was impressed by the holistic history, linguistics, and archaeology of the region as it is being developed by the so-called Minimalists in Israel and the West. Also, though they were not so aware of its destructiveness, the cosmic quantavolution that transformed the Late Bronze into the Iron Age helped me to picture well the conglomerate of peoples of the region and how they changed with the universal destruction that occurred then. The peoples of Canaan were linguistically, geophysically, and genetically related.

Jews everywhere today have unique genes in common with the Palestinians (and Arabs), even after 2000 years of miscegenation among many other peoples. I bring up this genetic factor not to espouse racism, but rather to show how far back Arabs and Jews have shared a special blood relationship, back to Canaan. This is said, in turn, to shunt aside all those spoilers of human relations who have made racists of many Israelis. Granted, our theory is a kind of racism too: Semitic racism. But in a technical sense, without bellicose and discriminatory conclusions.

❖ ❖ ❖ ❖

My Canaan proposal seems to ask of Israelis and Palestinians so much in the way of change that the new name may appear to slight the two peoples who are to dwell harmoniously in the same State of the Union. But we bank on its being a likable name. And we worry that the name Israel-Palestine might nurse factionalism. Neither the Czech nor the Slovaks were ever comfortable with the name "Czechoslovakia."

I felt relieved when I came upon a small political and literary circle of Jews who thought of themselves not as Israeli nor even as Jews but as

"Canaanites," whose language was Hebrew in its original form related to the Bronze Age dialects so far as they could be discovered. And, although their politics failed them, their idealism did not, and I found in them precisely the attitudes of Canaanite holism – incorporating Philistines, Phoenician, and other nations of the region from Lebanon to the River of Egypt and East to beyond the Jordan River. They believed in an original Semitic Hebrew dialect and people, but not in an Israel or religion of Judaism as their roots, and they dismissed Zionism and the Diaspora Jews as the preferred rulers of the land.

In brief, the land belonged to its inhabitants, which were pre-Zionist, but certainly included the Palestinians. Baruch Kurzweil, an interpreter of the movement, believed that a political ideology for the region would come from the Canaanites. But the effects of the Shoah on the Zionists and then on the Israeli psyche countermanded this prospect. It brought an obsessive event, a focus from Eastern Europe, a foreign (not indigenous) culture to dominate the Arabo-Hebraic Canaan root culture.

Another meaningful coincidence with my ideas is that the Canaanite movement saw the adjoining countries Syria, Jordan, Saudi Arabia, Egypt and Lebanon as culturally and geo-politically akin, and we have in mind with the advent of

31

THE AMERICAN STATE OF CANAAN

Statehood a blooming of friendly Arabic-USA boundaries. Statehood, indeed, would be a barrier to Israeli or American imperialism and allow a large step toward World Federation, possibly permitting a close cooperation between the whole of Europe, the USA and Western Asia. At one grand stroke such welcome probabilities occur. This vaguely fascistic but humanistic movement of Canaanites may thus therefore lend support to Statehood.

So, calling the new State of the United States "Canaan" and the new citizens by the same word "Canaans" to rhyme with "Kane'ens" would do well. (Popular usage would bring this about in any event.) The American States and populations go under Indian names or Spanish, French and British "noble" names. Maine, USA, is the "Maine" of France, Arizona is a Spanish dry region. Montana is for mountains. Georgian rebels hated George III. but, unlike the Russians who, after Stalin died, changed Stalingrad to Volgograd, they preserved the name of the bad, mad king. We schoolchildren where I lived sang lustily to the name of an extincted Illinois Indian tribe. The United States of America (USA) for a long time lacked an official name: "Columbia" came close to adoption. Then it would have been "Columbia, America," for the names of two Italian explorers. (*A propos*, in those days, Italy was the centerpiece of

European culture, yet was composed of a dozen small autonomous nations the size of Canaan.)

Canaans should recognize that the USA itself had no name, still has no name that it is entitled to, for there are many American States, some are federations, like Brazil, so these all could call themselves United States of America, could join in one big conglomerate Federation with a name ready-made, the United States of America - ranging from Nova Scotia to Tierra del Fuego. Therefore, if the most arrogant nation in the world can get to be the superpower without a proper name, there is no reason to spill blood so as to avoid a convenient, properly suggestive, ancient, historically comfortable, unclaimed name, that is, Canaan. So "Canaan" is logical, historically uniting Israelis and Palestinians.

Canaan would be true and would work, but had better not be a disputed issue. In the mass of Bible Protestants, it would be the only Biblical State name, so that fact should please a good many Americans. We would call them Bible Fundamentalists. Not surprisingly, many descendants from the Puritans see in Israel the original Israel, as do most Jews perhaps, at least officially. To many of these, an American State called "Israel" is only what should be expected. But the Palestinians derive from the Philistines of the

Bible and therefore, too, could claim the right to give their name to their new State.

Many opponents of Statehood may object primarily because of the change in name from Israel to Canaan. Understanding of course the need to oblige the Palestinians as well, and the liberty still fully available to use the name "Israel" for preserving the integrity of their religion, they may be mollified. Bible-readers will recall the story wherein Abraham, now Abram, is told by El Shaddai (to be translated as God Almighty), in Genesis 17:1-8, that he will be the father of many nations (plural) and these nations will be given by him "the whole of the land of Canaan." A strong claim is here established, to pursue the story, for Muslim Palestinian claims to Canaan, for they, too, claim Abraham (Abram) as their ancestor.

Actually, one could also debate whether the name of Israel is appropriate. The name derives from Jacob who had been "promised by Yahweh a magnificent land." One night a stranger came and wrestled with him until dawn, finally asking Jacob to let him go; Jacob obliged but demanded first to be blessed. The stranger would not give his name, is called only a 'man', not 'angel' or 'God,' but consented to bless him and said, "Your name will no longer be Jacob, but Israel, because you strove with God and with men and prevailed." *(The Torah*

CANAAN STATE, USA

and the Hafterot, in English and Hebew, trans and edited by Philip Birnbaum, publ.1983, Genesis 34:23-33.)

So Jacob became"Israel", and had twelve sons by two women, who became the chiefs of twelve tribes of Israelites. These twelve tribes did not stay united but Judah split from Israel, and became its bitter enemy. Judah exulted when Israel, a much richer nation, was conquered by the Assyrians and despatched into lands unknown. The Judeans made it quite clear, when writing and redacting the Bible afterwards, at home in Judah, then in their Babylonian captivity, and then back in Judah, that the disappearance from the Canaan region of the Israelites was good riddance of a pack of idolaters and polytheists of abased morality. If Yahweh were to be consulted, they would assure you, it would be apparent that he had changed his mind about giving the Israelites the promised land and because of their misconduct was turning it over to the Real Jews.

Well enough, but if many Israelis today want to keep their present state's name as the U.S. State name, everyone should know that the name "Israel" has in the Biblical stories both a promising side and a threatening side, and they will have to convince the Palestinians of their need, also muster American public opinion to let them prevail, and offend by their proverbial stubbornness those of us who are Canaans. Still, those who wish to be known

35

as Israelis, for whatever reason, may continue to be so known and addressed, and organized non-governmentally, leaving to those who decline the honor to be called Jews, atheists, Muslim, Baptists, Catholics, Orthodox or another name.

❖ ❖ ❖ ❖

Canaan would come into the Union with two peoples of differing income and wealth. The Israeli have destroyed or seized most of the wealth of the Palestinians and kept their jobs and incomes at a low level. The gap in income per capita between the two groups is 17 to 1 in favor of the Israeli. (This ratio can be compared with the USA to Mexico, which is far less, 4 to 1, or Germany with Poland, which is 3 to 1.)

Owing to Israeli inconsistencies of treatment, Palestinian poverty varies from bare subsistence to actual malnutrition. Some 70% of the population is usually below the poverty line. Now and then erratic policies raise the percentage for a short period of time. Based on household income, New Jersey USA, has only 6.8% of its population (still it counts 592,000 people) below the poverty line. Texas is worse off with 16.2% of its population below the poverty line (3,681,000 persons).

Thus, Palestinians are among the poorest people in the world. There is absolutely no natural or technical reason for this sad situation; it is entirely the consequence of Israeli policies, a fact which, considering the large number of decent, socially-minded Jews is almost incredible - save that we have the records at last of the full sixty years of a cruel elite. Unquestionably, were there a rule of law to combat massive repression in Israel, the condition of the Palestinian population would have been far better over the period of 60 years.

Canaan will have to adjust to new American law regarding ethnic discrimination. Jews were deeply affected, to begin with. Houseowners signed special clauses, prepared by realtors, to keep Jews out of a "gentile" neighborhood. Then, once they cracked this practice regarding themselves, after many court suits and a new reading of the U.S. Constitution, Jews were often as prompt as gentiles to sign up owners to prevent blacks from purchasing in a neighborhood, "to prevent everyone selling their house and moving out and wrecking house prices." All ethnic groups and poor "hicks" and "hill-billies" underwent milder resistance. But no more. Civil rights lawyers, Jews prominent among them, finally persuaded courts that such discrimination protocols were illegal, even unconstitutional. So the Canaans will be treated equitably when they buy property in America and - yes, for the Palestinians and Israeli Arabs - when they buy a house in a Jewish neighborhood. Which they will certainly do, just as Israelis are doing now in West Jerusalem, raising the same protests of "ruining the character of the neighborhood."

STATES FAR AWAY AND FAR OUT

The Republic of France was and is a centralized government whose prefects are usually the most powerful figures in the departments of equal size into which France is rather equally divided, exactly 100 of them. Yet all departments have elective legislatures. All towns have elective councils and mayors.

But, know this, too: of this one hundred quaint "Départements," four are situated overseas, as far as Tahiti, which is part of the Département of Polynésie Française, and is situated practically on the opposite side of the globe to the "mother-country." If you fly into Tahiti you can expect to be governed very much as you would be in Paris or Bordeaux, never mind the varied culture, honey-skinned people speaking a different language when they feel like doing so, and serving a cuisine that you might only be dreaming about at home. Tahiti is farther from Paris than Tel Aviv or Nome, Alaska, is from Washington, D.C. or Washington, D.C. from Honolulu, Hawaii. That is not all. One of the most active volcanoes in the world, the Piton de la Fournaise, is located in a French "Département," as well as the highest peak in the Indian Ocean, the Piton des Neiges, both in the Département of La Réunion, an island 700 km from Madagascar. There, as in Tahiti, you will find French "gendarmes," French state-owned tobacco shops, and on any day of the week, you can bet on horses at the local state-owned "bureau" of the PMU, off-track, in races to be run in Paris...

French and European rockets take off from the base of Kourou, in the French "Département" of Guyana, in South America, advantageously close to the Equator and permitting easy, optimal positioning of satellites. And Americans need not leave their continent to set foot on a French beach, be it on Guadeloupe or on Martinique. As for Saint Pierre-et-Miquelon, just a bit off Newfoundland but too small, with its 6,000 inhabitants, to be a French "Département," it has its own, somewhat lonely, prefect, and its school system depends from the rectorate of the Academy of Caen, in Normandy...

❖ ❖ ❖ ❖

Jokes were told about Jews who, though arrived in Jerusalem, still cried at the Wailing Wall because they wanted to go home to Miami. But Miami is only a day's journey from Jerusalem, where ancient prayers are fulfilled.

England lived off of India in part for over a century although New Delhi was far from London. And Russia today has the USA beaten, inasmuch as from St. Petersburg to Kamchatka, Russia's Easternmost "State," is a longer route than from Washington to Tel Aviv. American naval, air, and land forces are about as close to Israel as are Russia's. And Alaska, being the State furthest North, West and East, since it crosses the International Date Line, turns out to be only several hours farther by polar flight from Jerusalem than from Washington, D.C.

Almost instantaneous communication is now common and many forms of personal and group interaction and graphics exchanges as well. The Internet offers a hearty welcome to any new State. Israel is and Palestine could readily become (if Israeli soldiers were not nastily destroying much of their equipment donated by the European Union and others) typical infinite users of the Web.

41

THE AMERICAN STATE OF CANAAN

With the Internet, not only the large companies, but pop-and-mom shoe stores could operate branches in Seattle and the Gaza Strip.

Palestinian Freedom Fighters find an analogy in the Filipino fighters of 1899-1902. The United States had provoked a war with Spain and had attacked and destroyed the Spanish fleet at Manila Bay. A peace treaty was agreed to, whereby the United States had the choice of freeing the Philippines to become a nation-state or to govern them imperially. It chose to rule the Islands (It was President McKinley's decision to make and God told him he might do so, or so he said.)

Whereupon America found arrayed against it the same insurgents who had helped it to oust the Spanish regime. A prolonged bloody struggle followed, in which many thousands of Filipino fighters were killed, along with as many civilians, innumerable atrocities were committed, hundreds of villages destroyed, and the economy of the Islands disrupted and then usurped by American business interests. When America finally realized the futility of its actions, not to mention its immorality, it made peace with the rebels, let its hero, Aguinaldo, become its peacetime leader, and finally gave up fully its controls except for bases at Corregidor and Bataan, which fell to the Japanese aggressors soon after the Bombing of Pearl Harbor.

The Philippines were a much greater mass of lands and peoples as Israel-Canaan, nicely Catholicized and taught Spanish by their 300-year possessors. But here, the United States became embroiled in a Republican experience, penetrated hoggishly by American capitalists and owned still in good part by feudalists. It fought along the Americans in World War II, refusing to believe the Liberation propaganda of the racist Japanese. And afterwards received, with perhaps insufficient restraints, American aid and friendship. Filipinos fought with the Americans in Korea and Indo-China. English became the working language alongside Spanish and Tagalog. (We might notice in passing that both Hawaii and the Philippines endured a half-century of disorders prior to Statehood and independence.)

In the early 1800's, slave-holders of the American South, with the usual complement of wild-eyed politicians, buccaneers, investors, and military adventurers agitated to wrest Cuba from Spain – Cuba, "Pearl of the Antilles," a land of a rich and old culture, beyond any patch of the Old South. It did not happen. Else it would have given us by now a 30% black population, a richer Hispanic culture, and an even wider spread of Spanish as a second language than we have now. But the Cubans were already fierce and independent and would have fought for freedom like the Filipinos did a little later on.

COMPETING FOR POPULATION

A peopling crush is no great threat, whether militarily or electorally. Let us see why.

A great many American Jews and pre-Canaan Israelis resent the high birth rate of the Palestinians (just as many well-off gentile Americans disparage the higher birth rates of the poor). Israelis today are seized with panic at the thought that, unless they expel the Palestinians, they will soon be outnumbered by the offspring of the Arab mother whose fertility has generally been twice that of the Jewish mother, and furthermore, the Arab mother has her first infant several years ahead of her Jewish competitor.

The inability of most people to think properly in large numbers is quite common. Hitler had the German people, whose lower classes were among the world's best instructed, going into tantrums of fear and hostility over the Jewish presence. Yet there were in Germany, at that time, about 600,000 Jews, one in a hundred Germans.

The same panic causes self-defeating behavior. The more the state of Israel suppresses the Palestinians, the more prolific the Palestinian women will be, both in the camps and in Palestine itself. The positive correlation between malnutrition and childbearing is well-known. So is the correlation between poverty and unemployment on the one hand, and childbearing on the other. Increase the working-day population, raise the standard of living, raise women's education, and Arab women will bear less children.

If all the Palestinians of the refugee camps, the children and grandchildren of expelled forebears of 1948 and 1967 returned "home," Jews would be outnumbered substantially and within 30 or 40 years, Arabs would double their majority, it is said. Meanwhile, too, all things being equal, and unless they are integrated into Canaan, they will be even poorer, even less educated. Rapid birthing is not going to beat down Israel. It can only harm the Palestinian cause. In any event, no one has shown that any high-birthing class of people anywhere has thereby gained a critical victory in the struggle for power and welfare.

Professor Gunnar Heinsohn's "youth bulge" argument is that when a certain trigger percentage (e.g. 30%) of a population not locked into the security of prosperity and high employment are young men of fighting age (say 15 to 35), you can expect a range of activities from civil war to gangsterim to imperialism to terrorism. Deprived youth of every ethnic strain tend toward anti-social and disorderly conduct. (Heinsohn, though, does not help his case by citing as examples of countries led into war by their "youth bulges" two countries who suffered American invasions: namelu Iraq and Afghanistan.)

I remind Israelis of New Jersey, a rich State, almost the same size as Canaan, with great beaches and resorts and rich farmlands, and a population about equal to Canaan's, not counting Palestinian refugees. But will not a Palestinian preponderance defeat the Israelis in the upcoming elections in the State of Canaan? To comment a little ahead of time, the answer is no. There are many ways to capture policy-making in a state or country, or village, for that matter. What seems to be a solid majority by one criterion (cultural outnumbering) can turn out, because of factionalism, skilled campaigning, differential turnout rates in voting, etc. to fail appearing in the vote count. While making up nowhere even near a majority of voters, American Jews hold a substantial share of elective offices in the United States, probably four times the number that strict proportionality of offices to potential voters would provide.

THE AMERICAN STATE OF CANAAN

One of the numerous American Jewish-Israeli partnerships to keep Israel in tow has brought experts on apportionment and elections together from kept foundations and universities. Several clever tricks emerged. It was shown how appropriate statistical devices can turn a Jewish minority into a winning representation in a legislative body by manipulation of the boundaries of election districts, in short, gerrymandering, or violating the principle of equal-population-districts and contiguous boundaries, poorly but popularly termed "the principle of one man-one vote.".

Moreover, protected by the democratic institutions of the United States, and still endowed with enormous means of political and financial pressure, a Canaan State assembly with a small Arab majority would by no means represent a disaster for the Jews of Canaan, but quite to the contrary. The dynamics of well-backed opposition can be beneficial, intellectually and pragmatically, to a group. The Continental Christians who would eventually move to Canaan would probably give their votes to Jewish candidates.

Nor does a military machine emerge effectively from a crowd. A slight knowledge of military history will remind us of how a small well-equipped and disciplined army can defeat a large army of mediocre, even if brave soldiers. The Greek battles against the Persians in ancient times demonstrated the point on several famous occasions, even when the Greeks had inevitably to lose, as at Thermopylae. Repeatedly, in the American Civil War, a smaller Southern Confederate army would defeat a larger Northern States army.

A prize instance occurred sixty years ago when a Jewish militia in 1947-8, before there was an Israel or a proper Israeli Defense Army, defeated or at least effectively discouraged several Arab armies, including the highly touted British-led Transjordanian "Arab Legion," after and while burning down hundreds of Arab villages and turning out of their homes and country something less than a million Palestinian men, women, and children. In the conflict, the Jews demonstrated an organizing and coordinating ability, morale, and training, effectively mobilizing their small population, that were well beyond the capacities of the Arab countries. They were able , given the numerous "fronts," miscellaneous military units, haphazardly gathered and mis-assorted weaponry, to bring more combat soldiers and more firepower to bear at the critical scenes of engagement.

Moreover, a military threat to Canaan coming from its own Palestinian population appears like an absurd fantasy. Canaan, as an American State, would immediately become host to one, or several American military bases. Any threat

49

from outside (an almost unthinkable possibility) would be dealt with by the full military might of the USA and automatically involve the forces of NATO. In this secure territory, the Palestinian people would be reunited, safer than they have ever been, safer than any population in the Middle East. So would the Jews.

Under Statehood, a movement of people will no doubt take place. Reasoning statistically from what is scientifically known or surmisable cannot be reliable. Still, reasonable suppositions are better than assuming no movement at all or total displacement.

USA Population after Canaan Statehood.
(Date estimated 2010 - 2016)
Location of Population in Millions

US Citizens	In USA (excluding Palestinians)	In Canaan	In Middle-East	In Rest of the World
1.Muslim Palestinians	3.0	5.0	0.5	0.2
2.Jews	6.0	4.0	0.2	2.0
3.Christians	120.0	0.5	0.2	1.0
4.Secularists (not religious sectarian)	175.0	3.0	0.5	2.0

5.Religiously organized& controlled				
(Jews)	2.0	1.0	0.5	1.0
(Christians)	10.0	0.5	0.2	1.0
(Muslims)	2.0	2.0	1.0	2.0
TOTAL	318	16.0	3.1	9.2

The US has had so many shifts of and different melanges of population with declines and growths here and there, practically no phenotype of demographics is missing from its past and present. We should not expect, therefore, the Canaans to be upset or prone to reactivate enmities on this account.

A propos, the USA will hardly notice (at least not on the crowding side) the acquisition of 8 million new citizens who bring with them enough potential habitable land to handle 8 million secondary residences!

So, assuming our Israelis and Palestinians will accept the official designation of Canaan State (calling themselves whatever they might wish aside from their State name), we will disclose how many new Americans there will be. They now occupy, after the creation of Canaan, an area merely as large as the State of New Jersey and collect about the same-sized population, 8 millions. Their State is

51

also shaped rather like New Jersey and boasts a flat, sandy coastline as does New Jersey. Its back is to the Jordan River while that of New Jersey is to the Delaware River. And both States end where the ocean begins, the Red Sea and Delaware Bay in one case, the Mediterranean and the Atlantic Ocean in the other. Like New Jersey, Canaan, too, would be apportioned into counties centering upon some town or city.

The area of Canaan is 26,990 square kilometers, that of New Jersey 22,608 square kilometers. New Jersey counts 8,724,000 inhabitants. Canaan includes 3,762,000 Palestinians in its West Bank and Gaza areas, another 1,283,400 Palestinians who are citizens of Israel, and 2,859,000 refugees who are not let back by the Israelis but must be counted as citizens of the prospective State of Canaan. Other refugees, about 735,000 of them, are living around the world. The Palestinian refugees of course deserve the right to go home. The Israelis claim on behalf of Jews everywhere a promise of Yahweh and an ancient historic right to return to Israel, which they deny to Palestinians who have been evicted within the past few decades.

This historic "right" has no standing in international law, however. No more than an Italian, say, or a Swede, after 200 years in America, can claim the right to reenter Italy or Sweden on historical grounds. The world would be a strange place if the Greeks could go settle on the banks of the Euphrates or the Indus on account of Alexander the Great, or take over Sicily for the sake of Magna Graecia. Some 2,500 years do make a difference. The Sicilians are probably more racially akin to the Greeks and, mixed up well among themselves (including definitely an Arab strain) besides Siculi, Sicani, Phoenecian, Carthaginian, Greek, Roman (Italian), Norman, French, Spanish and German and the unlimited varieties of pirates, shipwrecked mariners, sailors jumping ship, myriad immigrants, and definitely Jews, before and after the rebellions against Rome, and during the Spanish centuries there. Still, they are genetically more alike than the Jews if a few drops of blood is what gives a ticket to Jerusalem or to Athens or to Syracuse. Actually, just about every ethnic strain in the world - from the Chilean Indian to the Ural Finn has such a right to a hundred different tickets. It's a smart Jew, or Swede, who can locate his Bronze Age hovel.

Population forecasting in Canaan includes a heated political struggle. Naturally the Palestinians seek every opportunity to exaggerate their numbers and fertility, while the Jews do the same. Hence the figures and estimates - past, present and future - are distorted on both sides, probably more so among the pro-Palestinian forecasters.

In fact, the Jews are all too willing to quote figures unfavorable to themselves in order to heighten the Israeli urge to bear more infants and to resist and reduce any charitable attitudes, and medical, alimentary, and welfare aid to Palestinian children, fooling themselves into thinking of Palestinian womanhood as a mere baby factory. One can notice, indeed, a deliberate reductive representation of Palestinian women in this regard, especially by distortion from Western media and the press, to deflect our own guilt for all the terrible deeds inflicted upon these unfortunate, largely blameless women, from the killing of their children and the tearing down of their homes on short warning (if there be a warning at all), to the daily hardship of unreliable and lengthily interrupted water and electricity supply, of near impossibility to visit relatives, or certain health facilities, or of simply feeding their families.

Whereas the Palestinian population is purely Arabic, the Israeli population is heterogeneous. Between 1948 and 1995, the number of Jewish immigrants entering from most sources of 10,000 or more are is shown on the following chart. Before 1947, immigration was largely illegal, pushed through by the threat of the concentration camp and the calloused unwillingness of Great Britain, the Arab countries and the North and South American countries to let in Jews in significant numbers and the refusal of the Axis countries to let them emigrate in any numbers.

In my special army unit in World War II, we numbered Jewish refugees from Italy, Germany, Austria, Algeria and Romania. I encountered a Jewish brigade from Palestine in the British 8th Army when I was a liaison officer working out of Mediterranean Allied Headquarters at Algiers. They seemed gloomy, as if they had little choice, or had no special assignments, and soon returned to Palestine, groomed for the war that loomed there.

Still, the quarter-million adult male Jews, desperate, fanatically intent upon expanding their foothold, could provide all who were needed to crush the ill-sorted coalition of Arabs that arose to meet them.

Between 1948 and 1995, the number of Jewish immigrants who entered Israel from countries sending 10,000 or more persons are carried on the following chart:

USSR and CIS	813,708
Morocco, Algeria, Tunisia	345,753
Romania	273,957
Poland	171,753
Iraq	130,302

Iran	76,000
United States	71,480
Turkey	61,374
Yemen	51,158
Ethiopia	48,624
Egypt, Sudan	37,548
Libya	35,865
France	31,172
Hungary	30,316
India	26,759
United Kingdom	26,236
Czechoslovakia	23,986
Germany	17,912
South Africa	16,277
Yugoslavia	10,141
Syria	10,078

.   The heavy influx of Russians to Israel is notable. With the Polish, Romanian, and American, they came to make up the majority and reinforced the Ashkenazi majority already in the country. They tended to associate with and serve the political and historical elements that related to the nineteenth century and pre-WWII immigrants, and who composed most of the ruling elite.

The Russian influx was not fully Jewish but contained a great many gentile partners, spouses, and simply fake Jews who wanted to get out of Russia, which was in a dreadful economic condition preceding, and especially following, the collapse of the Soviet Union.

Nor did the coming of the Russians, most of them impregnated with the atheistic culture of the Soviets, make the nation considerably more religious. About 1/3 of the Russian immigrants claimed to be atheists, in the same study that I used above. Fully formal Jewish conversions were uncommon, only 890 in 2002, for example, and 918 in 2003. Nor did assimilation move swiftly: only one-third of persons from the former Soviet Union declared that they had native-born Israeli friends.

Of the FSU immigrants, less than 1% chose to live in kibbutzim. Most sought the large cities, except Jerusalem – which apparently is too holy for the Russians, of whom only 1% were Orthodox Jews. They preferred crowded and costly Tel-Aviv, so Western in life style and with a flair of the Côte d'Azur to which Russians have legendarily been partial. But Tel-Aviv was too expensive for most of them. Over half of the Israeli- Jewish population live in the three substantial cities of Jerusalem, Tel-Aviv-Yafo, and Haifa. Worldwide, two thirds of the Jews live outside of Israel. Total Jews of the world are estimated at 13 million.

THE AMERICAN STATE OF CANAAN

Of total ex-Soviets who entered 1990-1 , 75,000 - or 22.5% moved internally within 5 years. Main motive was employment. Half stayed where they were, mostly because of family.

It is hardly known that the closeness of America and Israel owes much to the correspondence of ethnic origins between the American and Israeli Jews. I recall in New York overhearing an American tourist remarking to his wife in a Nebraska accent, reading his guide to the city, saying: "I didn't know that the Russians are the largest nationality group in New York."

There is today a continuous emigration from Israel, mainly to the United States, which posits the question whether the population can actually maintain itself. Many of the Russian Jews have used Israel as a trampoline to emigrate to the United States.

About half of a representative sample of Israeli said that if they were to be born again, they would prefer some other country than Israel. More exactly, 47% of the respondents, if born again, would prefer to be born elsewhere than in Israel (the Russian-born give us 70%), 62% of the wealthy sampling (born in Israel), 59% of the pensioners, 58% of the poor, 17% even of the Orthodox Jews! One might ask whether the world is being torn apart for the sake of an illusion, created by a few "true believers."

Under Statehood, we might expect a sea change. Jews in large numbers would exchange between Canaan and the Continental States. A heavy Palestinian emigration to the USA would occur. After the treatment they've been getting in Israel and the Arab states around them, they'll become 110% American in no time at all. Give them one (1) year.

That said about neighborhoods of the Canaans, can we guess where the new State's people would move over the range of America? Under Statehood, large movements of people affected will take place. Reasoning statistically from what is surmisable cannot be highly reliable, but takes us far from supposing no movement at all or total displacement, to a set of at least one likely outcome.

Americans on the average move every several years. Probably the Canaans will do the same. They have had little money and little permanent foreign alternative. If they did have these, they would have been like the Europeans in the nineteenth century, and would first move in large numbers (ca 200,000 per year) with ca 60,000 returning, depending mainly upon economic conditions.

Considering where they would settle, we can bet on over half of both immigrant Jews and Palestinians moving first to where relatives are,

59

then to where jobs exist, then to Texas, Florida and California, behaving, that is, like their predecessors. The total number of Canaans moving to the States would be about 2 million and of State-siders moving to Canaan would be about the same. In short, a balancing of populations.

A great deal of money exchanges, compensations, and material innovations would be accruing, which would affect who moves. Thus weapons workers would probably move disproportionately to the USA, while consumer industries and informatics would burgeon in Canaan.

If fertility rates for Israeli and Palestinian women remain for the next generation as they have been for the past generation (not counting immigration) the Israeli population of Canaan will remain the same while the Palestinian will double. As many Israelis emigrate as immigrate, so no important change seems likely in this regard.

Lately major changes have occurred in the fecundity of the populations concerned. The Palestinian rates have slumped while the Israeli have risen. The overall Palestinian birth rate has dropped from 7.57 in 1990 to 6.0 in 2000 to 3.4 in 2003. This change in only three years is spectacular. The Israeli rate of 2005 was 2.60. Jerusalem's rate was 3.95, the settlements rate in the West Bank was 4.70 and the Diaspora (abroad) rate was1.5. The women of Jerusalem in 2005 bore children in equal ratios: 3.94 for the Palestinians, 3.95 for the Israelis.

This startling change, studied by French demographers Emmanue Todd and Youssef Courbage, showed up throughout the Arab world, including Iran, but not Pakistan that was still a population bomb. Indonesia's fecundity rate has been dropping, too. The main reason for the low fecundity evidencing itself in the Muslim world seems to be the higher education of women, with a majority of university students in Iran now being women. Lower fertility correlates with literacy and education.

It can be assumed that Islam, far from being immune to secularization, is opening up. And women are leading the way, even with their heads covered. A major factor in the transformation is, of course, the mass media: television, films, electronic video and audio facilities of all kinds. It must be remarked also that Islam as a religion is less invasive of the private sphere in matters of fecundity than the Catholic Church. The frequently tragic experiences and the general social confusion and physical mobility of the Palestinian women add to the secularization effect and its accompanying small family. Canaan will have its Palestinian majority to begin with, still, and may go one way or the other once the population is accorded the mobility of American citizenship. But there will be

61

no peopling war, once the problem of the return of the refugees is solved. And in any event the problem of peopling including the return of the refugees will resolve itself readily within the great American Union.

STORIES OF ACHIEVING STATEHOOD

Numerous countries have severe separatist problems, Protestants from Catholics in Northern Ireland, Timor, Sri-Lanka, Scotland (from the United Kingdom), Corsica from France, Flemings from Walloons in Belgium, Basques in Spain. We know the tragic experiences of Yugoslavia, as Croatia, Bosnia, Montenegro and finally Kosovo were detached from Serbia, imitating the break-up of the Soviet Union. And, of course several separatist problems have confounded Russia itself, the worst of which has been the Chechen Republic where vastly outnumbered and outgunned Chechen have over many years, by so-called "terrorist" tactics and outright skirmishes, prevented Russia from imposing a peace at any price. Some types of extensive autonomy must in the end ensue, although Russia, lacking the true federalism of the USA, finds it difficult and not in keeping with its monolithic system to give true freedoms to the Chechens. (There is a question of oil, too!)

In Palestine, we find one of the worst problems of separatism of modern history. Great Britain, as mandatory Power, governed badly for a generation, then abruptly threw over its responsibility, withdrawing its forces and leaving Jews and Arabs in violent conflict. It wasn't the only case where the British, so adept at self-praise and at eliciting the praise of history-teachers, departed for "Old Blighty" leaving a political pot seething behind. In the partition of India into Muslim and Hindu states in 1947, leaving a geographic and religious mix-up, in which perhaps 20 million persons moved between what are now Pakistan and India, over half a million persons died in riots, massacres and hardships.

Belgium, whose cosmopolitan capital, Brussels, is the center also of the European Union, offers the distressing, perplexing problem of the society stretching in contradictory directions. The semi-Dutch Flemings, in good part, wish their own nation, although it is hard for the outside observer to understand what they lack in rights, liberties, style of living, education, etc. Except for the fatal name, *Der Staat.*

True, there is a historical inferiority feeling vis-a-vis the French culture of the Francophone

Walloons. But there is nothing at all like the gaps that exist and grow between Israelis and Palestinians. As with Alsace, France, that has generally accommodated both German (Alemanic) and French culture, Belgium has enjoyed two highly creative and respected cultures, with possibly the Francophone the more prestigious, at home and abroad. Should the two peoples stupidly divide, in the name of nationalism, it will be unfortunate and costly but probably not fatal. In the end, the Flemings' culture and society will probably decline, drifting away from the great abstraction of the European Union, with its "inside story" and thousands of Frenchified jobs and non-governmental Francophone organizations. A common view of the intelligentsia is that of the sculptor Wim Delvoye: "I am a Belgian artist and Dutch is my first language. But I do not want any regional power that forces me to be a 'Fleming.' I want to remain a compatriot of Magritte, Ensor, Rops or Amélie Nothomb."

❖ ❖ ❖ ❖

The 50 United States of America originated variously. From private tracts of land, Lord Delaware's, came a sovereign State of the Confederation, this being a group of independent sovereignties, who gave up certain rights and powers, but not the critical power to withdraw or to dissent and be excepted from a law of the others. The Confederation was a "League of Nations," or a "United Nations" in this regard.

Not only Delaware, but twelve more "Provinces" and "Colonies" formed the United States under the Constitution, whose major departure from the prior Confederation was the agreement to be ruled by the whole body, assembled in a bicameral Congress and served by an indirectly elected President and an appropriate Supreme Court.

Then came the batch of new States. First came the Vermont Republic patched from a New Hampshire grant and New York province. In 1792 Kentucky County was cut from Virginia; Tennessee from the Southwest territory of North Carolina; Ohio from the Northwest territory of the United States Government. Although admitted as a State in 1803, it happened not to possess an act of admission until Congress got around to declaring such in 1953! Massachusetts gave up land to constitute a State of Maine.

President Jefferson extralegally (no such power was given the action under the Constitution) purchased the vast 2-million-square-kilometer "Louisiana Territory" from Napoleon Bonaparte of France in 1803 at a price that amounted finally to about $22,000,000.

Its southern part became the "Orleans Territory" in 1804 and in 1812 became the 18th State, Louisiana. It was a bilingual area, with the South mostly Francophone and the North Anglophone.

Then came a group of four more States that had briefly been territories surveyed out of the Louisiana Purchase.

Florida emerged from a trade of western land rights with Spain, and was admitted in 1845. So, too, Texas in 1845. Then several territories from the Midwest and Oregon in the Far West, after a near war with Great Britain over its boundary with Canada, while wild Americans were rushing about crying "54o40' or Fight." Kansas was admitted in 1861 in the middle of an undeclared war between Northern "Free Staters," and slavery sympathizers, "Bleeding Kansas" it was called.

Meanwhile California had revolted from Mexico, became a short-lived "Grizzly Bear" Republic, and was admitted in 1850. Iowa, Wisconsin, and Minnesota advanced from Territory to State uneventfully. But in the middle of the fierce Civil War, an anti-slavery force rebelled from Virginia and, calling themselves West Virginia, were brought into the Union, one of a number of unconstitutional actions taken by Lincoln and the exclusively Union-dominated Congress in 1863. Nevada the next year, Nebraska,

Colorado, North and South Dakota, Montana, Washington, Idaho, Wyoming and Utah, all territories by hook or crook, in the years 1864 to 1896.

A pause in Statehood occurred during which the USA seized Puerto Rico and the Philippines from the tired Empire of Spain. Oklahoma was the next State, an amalgamation of Indian tribal territory and the Territory of Oklahoma.

❖ ❖ ❖ ❖

Let us continue for a moment with the Oklahoma story. The "Clovis" spearhead and mound-building cultures prospered there, eating mammoth steaks, thousands of years ago, well before the Hebrew and Arabs were known as such. The white man appeared at the end of the 18th century along with the Osage and the Quapaw nations. Then came the Five Civilized Tribes, voluntarily moving away and otherwise expelled by the whites. They set up boundaries and independent governments in and around Oklahoma. The Civil War embroiled the Indians. They were invaded from all sides by other Indians and by Northern and Southern white troops and free-booters.

The Five Civilized Tribes attempted to form a United States but were opposed by "Big Brother" USA, which forced them to make a State of themselves within the Union, the 46th, Oklahoma, in 1905. (It is conceivable that an unspeakably determined America could force Palestine and Israel to become the State of Canaan "for the good of the whole world which is under dire threat from these incorrigibles.") Presently some 67 Tribes call Oklahoma their home, a quarter of a million Indians live there, and many Tribal Councils carry on their own local governments. Note well: at least five complete little nations, modern style (a Cherokee had even invented a writing system), came to life and existed in the middle of the United States.

The New Mexico and Arizona Territories became States in 1912 and finally Alaska and the Territory of Hawaii were admitted in 1959, by which time this author had been raised to an age when he might participate in the agitation over the admission of the State of Hawaii.

❖ ❖ ❖ ❖

Only a rare American knows the list of admissions to Statehood or can even remember their names. Israeli or Palestinians need not memorize them either. Canaans, in fact, since they will be made citizens *en bloc,* need prove no knowledge of American history, unlike ordinary immigrants applying for citizenship.

Canaans will take a large leap forward (backwards?) into 21st century culture, especially popular culture and consumer culture. What can be called American exportable culture began already after the First World War in the 1920's to spread over the world, a kind of "soft imperialism" which, barring catastrophe of one kind or another, will continue indefinitely into the future as the "Primary Cultural Globalism."

In this, our broad perspective on world cultural development, the Israel-Palestine State will be a readily adapted contributory element to "Primary American Globalism." Will long dresses return to womanhood with the garb of several million Muslims; will American women go back to wearing special hats as funny as they were a hundred years ago? Doubtless there will simply be more and more of the merging and assimilating that has gone on for so long in the United States.

A foremost American historian, Professor Charles Beard, wrote a book a century ago entitled *An Economic Interpretation of the Constitution of the United States of America,* where he showed how the Constitutional Convention was convened under false pretenses, how the financial interests of the

Founding Fathers were heavily protected by its provisions (including the slavery interest), and how the not very popular idea of taking sovereignty away from the Confederate States was promoted and the voting manipulated to produce the required approval of the Document describing the new frame of government.

Charles Beard did not catch all the peculiarities of American history in the subsequent histories that he wrote together with his wife, Mary. Not until another century passed, was the little matter of the nation itself not having a name illuminated, this time by a Political Scientist, Sebastian de Grazia, in a work entitled "A Country without a Name."

So if the potential citizens of the State of Canaan fear that they will be rushed into incompleteness and oversight while getting into the Union, they can cite many queer and roguish elements in American history - which have not ended by any means.

But the poor white population would never tolerate giving the former slaves benefits which they themselves did not receive. And the North was a booming enterprise where the poor and the working class also received low wages and few other benefits.

In the "Palestinian" South, therefore, neither politics nor economics worked. White and black both were exploited and held in contempt by the Northern elite. America's politics and development thereupon for eighty years was a disgusting spectacle of rampant individualism. Northerners were like the Israeli, regarding Palestinians. They had little idea of most conditions in the South and indeed were blinded by puritan hypocrisy and scandalous mythogenic media in their own States.

❖ ❖ ❖ ❖

The State of Utah also had remarkable beginnings. Like many of the States it had troubles at the start and collected other troubles before becoming a State. The Mountain Meadows Massacre of 1857 tells us something. The Mormons, properly nervous from past religious persecution before emigrating, received reports that a Federal army was approaching, sent by President Buchanan, a fool excited by Mormon-haters, to implant a garrison in their community and treat them as traitors. The Mormons, already armed, prepared for possible combat with the United States.

At the same time, a large wagon train of immigrants from the troubled South (with Confederates) was fleeing their country for the

"Golden West." They passed near a Mormon settlement which, persuading Indian friends to take up arms as well, massacred the emigrants at Mountain Meadows (September 11, 1857). Brigham Young and the Elders North in Salt Lake City heard of the slaughter and hushed it up. Years later, a principal in the episode was punished, and the Mormon community as a whole suffered national scorn. Some thought the massacre was revenge for the way they had been treated in Missouri and Illinois. Texas was settled by Spaniards who miscegenated with the 20 or so tribes of the three greater peoples: Pueblos, Mound Builders, and Mexicanos. All except four of them have disappeared by now as societies. Texas had already a separate status when Americans from the South began to infiltrate, actually with some encouragement from the Mexican authorities, bringing with them slaves . Mexico had banned slavery in 1804. German and Alsatian contingents entered the country as well, moving towards the center. (Even today the ethnic German heritage accounts for 10% of the population of Texas of 20 millions, a little larger than the British with 7 % and the Scots-Irish also with 7%.)

The immigrants from the USA found ample grievances besides having to hide their slaves from the authorities, mainly a corrupt bureaucracy, so, together with some Mexican neighbors, revolted against the Mexican government, succeeding in 1836 to become the Republic of Texas. Soon a movement to become an American State gathered strength and 1845 saw Congress passing a resolution annexing the Republic.

Shortly thereafter the Texas Constitution was modified and approved by Congress as the basis for Statehood. (Slavery was explicitly authorized therein.) And before the year was out, Texas had become a State, by far the largest in size, though still small in population.

However, Mexicans, mainly mestizo (Indian-Spanish) became an oppressed minority. The power, wealth, and aggressive willingness to use force of all kinds, given the negligence of the mestizos and paucity of Spanish Mexicans, produced two peoples, like Israelis and Palestinians, living side by side as citizens, but very unequal in actual rights and welfare. Only after the populations grew hugely and a spirit of due process of law and equality suffused the Hispanics, did they bestir themselves. They grew in numbers to 36.5% by 2006 and came to occupy an ever larger number of official positions and a higher assimilated status in society and state. Still 1.2 million were illegal immigrants. But in a matter of time, they would by their higher birthrate as well as by immigration, both legal and illegal, come to form half of the population.

Although the analogy with Palestinians and Israelis applies, no major revolts or terrorism occurred. Like America in general, instead, personal violence and gangs disturbed the peace. The jails were well-filled. Much of this resulted from personal, racial and ethnic hostilities.

Withal, Hispanic or not, Texans generally demonstrated a satisfaction with their mode of life and an exorbitant pride in their State. There is little reason to believe that this same condition could not prevail in Israel-Palestine, tolerable and improving, that is, even become constructive, cooperative, creative and productive, including a Canaan equivalent to "Tex-Mex" culture becoming popular around the States.

In the Civil War, Texans voted heavily with the South for secession and slavery, did not see heavy warfare during the War but then underwent a typical, even worse, period of trouble during the Reconstruction and even far into the Twentieth Century.

What happened in the Reconstruction and Redeemer Period in the USA Southern States, in Texas and elsewhere, must be avoided in the State of Canaan. A full program of rights, and all the needed machinery and will to enforce them, must go into the intent, wording and activation of the Constitution and administration of the Fifty-first State.

We would not carry the feeble territory of Palestine into the Union as it is, but would be obliged to guarantee its powers and privileges as equal to the Israeli ones. Not necessarily stopping there. There is good reason for carrying in the new State Constitution not only all the privileges of citizens of the most civilized States of the Union but also the laws that have been most importantly enacted to support the federal Constitution.

Thus the Constitution of Canaan should not only carry the bill of rights and other part of the federal constitution, repeating them, but repeating also the prominent laws of enforcement and reinforcement. For example, a model clause calling for "affirmative action" for citizens of the new State might be included in its constitution.

Now this brings us to an important query. What Territory, if any, was admitted to the United States fully virtuous? None whatsoever. In fact, putting aside only several of the States that wrote and promoted the Constitution, a notable complement of wickedness was evident. Notwithstanding, they were admitted to the sounding of patriotic songs and proud beating of drums. So will it be with Canaan.

❖ ❖ ❖ ❖

Hawaii has two official languages, English and Hawaiian. Japanese is often spoken, too. The percentage of Hawaiian residents who speak Hawaiian is less than the percentage of Israelis who speak Hebrew, and of course all Palestinians speak Arabic. Several states are moving towards adopting Spanish as a second language. Thus there is precedent for the Government of Canaan to adopt three languages as official - English, Hebrew and Arabic. Of course, many Americans would consider this a bad precedent for America - all those who want English to be the official language and insist that there be no incentives for a Spanish speaker to become bilingual. It is shameful that the United States, with a plethora of various linguists feeding into its culture for four hundred years, has contemptuously reduced to a paltry percentage its multi-linguists.

Hawaii is the most remote from a continent of any considerable island. It is 2300 miles (3700 km) from the mainland, thus about 6500 miles from Washington. Hawaii was admitted to the Union in 1959 after many years of controversy. Several large agricultural and shipping corporations, descended mainly from Christian missionaries, ran the government of what was made into the Territory of Hawaii by Congress. This followed a *coup d'état* in which the white settlers, who should have been content with being rich and happy in the sacred volcanic islands, deposed the Queen.

Hawaii is one of four States that were independent prior to Statehood, together with California, Texas and Vermont. It was an Independent Republic from 1894-8. Annexed by the US in 1898, it became officially a Territory in 1900. The UN Charter contained special provisions for guarding non-independent countries, into which group and to American surprise, Hawaii fell. The US had therefore, ignominiously in some American eyes, to fill out an annual report to the UN Assembly on its conduct. It did so from 1946 to 1959.

An administrative Act was passed by both Houses of Congress and signed by the President. Thereupon a referendum was called whether to accept the Statehood being offered. The vote went 17 to 1 in favor. Of its population of 1,275,000 (2005), Asians compose 57.33%, Native Hawaiians 22.1% and mixed races 20%. Ethnic and racial friction is minimal. Persons who are in part Native Hawaiian are likely to boast of the fact.

Hawaii, that beautiful and productive State, was said by a great many to be unfit for Statehood. It had for one thing 80% of so-called foreign races – not only the burly dark and supposedly incompetent Polynesian natives, but almost half a people of Japanese origin, rather less Chinese and

Filipino, then many Portuguese and a variety of Euro-oriental mestizos. A few *haoles* (white mainlanders) ran the show and kept the books. Some naval vessels and a garrison stood by somnolently until exploded into action by the surprise Japanese air and sea attack of December 7, 1941.We must admit, though, that they all loved Hawaii. And had suffered a defeat by "terrorist" attack so devastating and threatening to the whole Pacific Region that it diminishes the enormity of the disaster of the World Trade Center. There was talk of abandoning the Islands as being indefensible, especially in view of the main war going on in Europe.

Hawaii became a confused and befuddled and crowded place with four sets of rulers, each hoping to rid itself of the others: the communist-flavored-labor union movement mainly of longshoremen and seamen that enveloped, too, the great San Francisco Bay Area, and could tie up the whole Western flank of the United States and Canada at will; the old white (tinged with Polynesian brown and Chinese) owning and management class who were rich and well content; the Japanese who though docile, efficient and the backbone of the working class, were quite aware of the potential of civil rights and capable, as was shown in World War II, of fighting in an army, and afterwards of running a country. The Navy could be deemed a fourth aspiring ruling group determined to run a clean, anti-radical, anti-union, Washington-directed operation. So liberal the outlook of the country socially, though, or, let us say, laissez-faire, that individuals of every stripe and color went their way prosperously or on the beach.

So there were the oligarchs, the quasi-imperial Japanese, the labor radicals, the Navy, and the happily mongrelized 20% besides. In every group, there were many who resisted Statehood, either because they would rather rule the roost themselves as a Territory, or step out boldly as an independent country, or perceived the evil social changes that would overcome the blessed islands, once granted Statehood, even if their life style lay in the shore pleasures of the wandering sailor or in driving the lackadaisical Hawaiian natives into a strict Christian puritanism.

❖ ❖ ❖ ❖

Alaska was seized by Russians in 1733, who held it until 1867 when it was sold to the USA for a trifle and converted into a Territory in 1912 which extended from its vast bulk both East along the string of Aleutian Islands to Asia and South along the Pacific Coast practically to the US border.

A few Alaskans still speak Russian, 5% the native tongue and the balance of its 627,000 inhabitants speak English. It is organized in boroughs, not counties. No matter. Half of its land is owned by the Federal Government and held for conservation purposes, unlike the large land holdings of the Israeli Government that are accumulated in order to take it out of Palestinian hands.

Political parties are easy to found in Alaska: the 25 parties at last count outnumber even those of Israel. Several are radical workers' parties but these and the other dozen or so parties slump into the Democratic and Republican parties come national elections. On occasion, a third party will flash out. A State's Independence Party (libertarian, privatizing, against conservation) calls for secession and claims that international law was violated in not permitting a vote on independence. Founded in 1984, it actually elected a Governor (Hickey) in 1990.

All of its glaciers are melting, as is the ice of the sea coast, so Alaska is enlarging or shrinking, depending upon how you look at it. Its offshore oil deposits are becoming more accessible, and trouble is already brewing over the rights to extract it among Russia, Norway, Greenland, Canada and the USA.

Alaska was a simple case, a land purchased for a few million dollars from Czarist Russia, a land one-fifth the size of the United States, a land not yet known to be rich in oil though its fisheries were already exploited and its timber would soon be. And as wrongly the Zionists said about Palestine, "there are no Palestinians, there where we are going," one might rightly say that there were no native Alaskans – less than Palestinians by far, under a hundred thousand Indians and Inuit (Eskimos) and a few Russian, Canadian, American, and other isolates. Most were quite poor, as poor and proud as Palestinians. The territory was completely exploitable, but with too few exploiters at first to matter. But then came the big gold rush, timber exploiters, the oil diggers, the Oil Carriers, including the *Exxon Valdez* ruination of whole villages and rich fishing waters with its grounding off the Alaskan Shore.

No matter how absurdly contrived the agenda of Congress, there is always room for more games. It was time to talk Statehood. Four powerful Senate seats and three House seats were up for grabs. Most Republicans thought they would capture a State of Hawaii, whereas the Democrats would gain Alaska. So both thought they had reason to balk. President Eisenhower spoke up for Hawaii but wanted Alaska held up until certain extensive provisions for its defense could be settled. Racist Southern Democrats, led by Senator and President-to-be L.B. Johnson, blocked multiracial Hawaii. So all was held up until both could be admitted as States at the same time and they were, in 1959, by a bipartisan group in Congress. And both States elected representatives of mixed party affiliation. Which State got the better representation in its legislature, in Congress, and from the bureaucracy that managed so much of their resources would be hard to tell without a research effort impossible here.

❖ ❖ ❖ ❖

There was nothing particularly virtuous about these States, their peoples or their activities that would have them embraced by Statehood. Less and worse can be said about most of the States that have been allowed in or back into the Union from 1789 to 1914. Let us make up a quiz: Would you like to have a State that enjoys and enforces human slavery? If not, you might not wish to have been part of the United States in the first place, and certainly not in the latter part of the Nineteenth Century when slavery had been abolished everywhere but in its homeland, Africa, and some Islamic countries. For, in the United States, after a period that should be pronounced derisively

"Reconstruction," in order to elect a man named Rutherford Hayes President, the election being so close as to be thrown into the House of Representatives for a decision, a horrendous bargain was struck that enabled the most racist and corrupt elements of several southern States to throw out several partially recomposed and constitutionally forward-looking State governments.

Thus it was, after 250 years of outright slavery of millions of Americans, five years of warfare as murderous as any that had been known to the world for some time, there occurred twenty years of slowly moving reform toward providing human rights to a tenth of the population (we will not speak here of the brutal treatment of the Chinese in California, of the Mexicans throughout the Southwest, and of the mass of immigrants in the East where Jews worked all the long day in stifling factories at piddling wages, and Welsh and Italians worked in coal mines that were often collapsing. (While testifying before a Congressional investigating committee, a mine-manager jested about the cost advantages of "more wops and less props.")

No State west of the Mississippi was admitted to the Union without a scary record of lynch law, gang wars, raving gunmen, alcoholism, industrial warfare in the factories and in the mines all over the land, ethnic and racial rancor, and Indian suppression ("the only good Indian is a dead Indian" remarked the famed hero General Philip Sheridan in 1869) - all of this was prevalent in the last twenty or more States to be admitted up to Arizona in 1914.

Then came the period from World War I to World War II, 1914 to 1945, and America was still not heavily engaged in the Near East. The last sixty-five years, however, have seen a heavy US involvement, brought on at least in appearance because of the concerns of Israel, International Jewish organization, and American Jews, although the diminished roles of the French and British empires in the region, the American need for petroleum, and the Cold War against the USSR increased American engagement as well.

ZIONISM AND A GAGGLE OF SCHEMES

At the time of early Zionism, nationalism and imperialism were movements in full swing. Italy, the USA, and Germany, all three of which had imperial pretensions, were raiding Africa, Asia, wherever they could seize a colony, whatever was left over from the more advanced predators, Portugal, Spain, Britain, France, the Netherlands, Belgium. Italy attacked the failing Ottoman Empire. The USA was goading the dying Spanish Empire. Germany did not come upon choice territories: Southwest Africa, for example, proved hopelessly poor.

In Germany the idea became popular of taking over, instead, new contiguous *Lebensraum* ("living space") in the vast Eastern plains and the Balkans, stirring the *Drang nach Osten* ("drive to the

East"), soon clad in sultry racial mysticism: hadn't the whole Indo-European race come from the Central Asian steppes?

Another dynamic, equally important to the birth of Zionism, was the reworking in depth of the geopolitics of Central Europe: the constitution of independent nation-states, either through centripetal forces, by aggregating units that were formerly separated, and of different status, as in the formation of Italy or Germany, by then successfully achieved; or by centrifugal forces, detaching national units from larger aggregates, the Austro-Hungarian Empire and the Ottoman Empire.

Although Theodor Herzl, (1860-1904) Founder of Zionism, himself was born in Budapest, his family originated from Semlin, a small town in Serbia. Serbia had recently, after a lengthy struggle, achieved independence from the Ottoman Empire (but was prevented by the Austro-Hungarian Empire from unifying with Bosnia and Montenegro). It was in this town of Semlin that, in 1857, in the middle of the struggle of Serbia for independence, and inspired by the event, one local Rabbi, Judah Alkalai, wrote a book prescribing the "return of the Jews to the Holy Land and the renewed glory of Jerusalem." The rabbi was a friend of Herzl's grandfather. The book garnered little attention in its time, but was handed down to Herzl – as well, no doubt, as Rabbi Alkalai's memory and ideas – by his grandfather. The term "Zionism" itself was coined after the hill of Zion in Jerusalem, where the first Temple may have stood, by Nathan Birnbaum, a Jewish journalist, in 1890; adopted by Herzl, the name and idea caught on quickly enough to inspire a large First Congress of Zionism in Basle in 1897.

Zionism, therefore, combined the ideologies of European colonialist expansion and of European nationalism. Like both of these, it drew upon, and justified itself with notions of "progress," "enlightenment," "human brotherhood", and a conviction of European superiority. It also pparticipated in the social utopianism of the times.

By the end of the 19th century, Jews were fully aware that they could match man-for-man the full range of individual capabilities of Westerners and could well imagine themselves administering a state as well as a business enterprise. Disraeli, after all, ran the British Empire for Queen Victoria. Jews even had a tremendous religious card, if it could be controlled - Judaism. Wherever they went, they would find, if not a Jewish family in Diaspora, some sympathizers introduced by the Bible, in whatever language and version.

Jewish contacts were as worldwide as the Jesuits' and the Freemasons'. (Apropos, from 80,000 to 200,000 Freemasons were murdered by the Nazis as cooperators with the Jews and hostile ideologues.) Men like Herzl believed that they had to pull their act together. They needed a base of operations, a homeland, a Vatican – Palestine if possible, but even Uganda (for no special reason except spaciousness) came under consideration. And later on, Josef Stalin would provide a Jewish Homeland in Asia, an Autonomous Jewish Oblast of Birobizhan, at the Chinese border, in which the Soviet Jews could pursue their "Yiddish cultural heritage." Birobizhan was not, however, destined to be a center for regrouping the world's Jews.

As for Herzl, the German Kaiser himself, whom Herzl visited twice, considered lending a hand. Under the influence of his relative, the Grand Duke of Baden, a practitioner of spiritism, the Kaiser had devised a bizarre scheme whereby Germany would wrest control of Palestine away from his own English royal relatives, and await the Second Coming of Christ, which both he and

Baden thought was nigh, so that he, the Kaiser, would have the honor of being host to this illustrious returning visitor in a now German-owned Jerusalem. Herzl seemed to fit into the plan.

The United States itself were already ahead of the Zionist idea, with its own supply of "Jews" in the form of dissident Protestant sects bent upon reenacting the Bible, who originated a score of Promised Lands, begun according to Biblical specifications: Seventh Day Adventists, Mormons (Church of the Latter Day Saints), Jehovah's Witnesses, and so on, going back to the 17th Century "Pilgrim Fathers" of Plymouth, Mass.

Herzl's Zionists were typical romantic nationalists of the late nineteenth century, wanting what was then fashionable to want, a real "state" permitting one to wave one's very own flag, to the sound of a national anthem evoking the overture of "Tannhaueser..." They were not especially moral or religious. Indeed, some of them, including Herzl, would settle for a decent piece of land that they could call Jewish no matter where it was. As I said, Protestant America had already a goodly share of Promised Lands, but they were not real Jews. If historically Jews had longed to return to Palestine, there would have been better occasions over the past 2000 years. Actually, there had been a large, influential and wealthy Jewish voluntary "Diaspora" around the greater Mediterranean region centuries before the Jews were expelled from Roman Palestine in AD 72; the Babylonian Captivity, early Sixth Century BCE, could be used as an early date of the Diaspora.

We should ad, at this point, that if recent historical research has shown that the land of Canaan had never been in war and bloodshed by Joshua bin Nun, and that the Hebrews were its autochtonous, peaceful inhabitants, even more recent historical research has shown that the Romans never deported and chased the Jews from the Land of Israel nor caused their scattering around the world where they remained in exile for 2,000 years. The Romans did destroy and loot the Temple, and this destruction was and remains the fundamental trauma. But no deportation took place.

In fact, archaeology shows that some thirty years after the supposed expulsion, cities in Palestine and their synagogues were thriving. This fact is not unknown to Jewish historians: fifty years later, another considerable Jewish uprising took place in Palestine. Again, there were no mass expulsions or dirving away of people from the land. If anything, Judaism knew in the following two centuries a "golden age" of prosperity and cultural development in Palestine. The myth of exile and scattering was, at least in part, an invention of the Christians who were intent on convincing themselves, and the Jews living among them, that God had punished and abandoned them, that they were no longer the Chosen People.

But why, then, were these Jews living in considerable numbers among them? The fact is that from the 6th Century B.C.E., important Jewish communities had been living in Persia, and that by the 4th Century B.C.E. they were living in large numbers in the Hellenic world, speaking many languages, but especially Greek (the earliest version of the Bible was written down in Greek), that their communities, often wealthy, spread all around the Western Mediterranean and the Roman world, a result of emigration but also, and this is where the new historical research comes in, of widespread conversion. Important communities were established in Egypt and Southern Spain long before the destruction of the Temple by the Romans.

ZIONISM AND A GAGGLE OF SCHEMES

Monotheism had a profound intellectual appeal to the Greco-Roman world, which was moving with philosophical logic towards atheism. Largely from the trauma of the Temple destruction, sprang a messianic belief in an avenger who would be sent by God to Jerusalem and rebuild it. But rabbinical commandment forbade to hasten the coming of the Messiah, and even for the Jews, to establish themselves in Jerusalem: the place became for them sacrally taboo, as it became holy to Christians and then to Muslims.

What happened, then, to the Hebrews of Palestine? Most of them converted to Islam in the 7th and 8th century AD. While a little later, in the Caucasus and around the Caspian Sea, the powerful people of the Khazars converted wholesale to Judaism, and became spread out to what is today Ukraine. From them, evidence seems to shows, descend most of the Hews from Eastern Europe. Jewish communities existed by then all the way to India and China. Many of the Jews, over time, from Bagdad to the Caucasus to Egypt moved to and became settled in their historically most glorious homeland, Andalusia. It is a much more fascinating story than the reductive one of wrteched tribes of exiles invented by the contemptuous Christians... I recommend reading the book of Israeli historian Shlomo Sand: "How the Jewish People was Invented."

For centuries, it can be argued, the Jews were more secure in Islamic lands than they were in Christian Europe. The ancient Sephardic Jewish communities of Spain were subjected to continuous religious suppression by the early Christian church and were "liberated" by the Moors' invasion of Southern Spain in 711. In fact the Jewish communities aided the establishment of the Moors and their advances further North. Thus came to be created the most brilliant civilization of its time on European soil. Although Jews were of a subordinate status to the Muslims, their communities thrived in Spain, and Jews from all parts of Europe and Asia, from Morocco to Babylon, came to join their brethren in Andalusia.

If we are to acknowledge the crudity of the crumbled remains of the sites of Biblical Israel, as unearthed by Israel Finkelstein and others, Andalusia may have been the best homeland the Jews ever had, culminating in the Jewish "Golden Age" of the Twelfth Century. And the Jews' expulsion - along with the Moors' - in 1492, under the orders of Isabelle-the-Catholic, Queen of

Castille, after Muslim Spain had fallen to the Spanish, was the fundamental trauma of modern Jewry, more than the long-past expulsion from Jerusalem.

Again, it was the Muslim Ottoman empire which opened its lands to the Jewish refugees and gave them yet another "Jerusalem:" the city of Salonica in the North of Greece, close to the center of power of Istanbul, which became within a generation the largest Jewish city in the world. Until its extermination by the Nazis in World War II, this Jewish community still spoke *Ladino,* a language marrying Spanish and Hebrew, which had originated in pre-Moorish times in Spain.

It is deeply wrong to minimize the innumerable occasions in history when the Jews (always a minority) were persecuted, mildly (but is there such a thing as mild persecution?) or terribly. It is misleading, though, to enumerate historic persecutions against Jews to the exclusion of the persecution of other groups, creating the notion that "the whole world" was "always" against the Jews, and only against the Jews. The Papacy's crusade against the Albigensian Cathars (and the non-Cathar population) of Southern France must be the worst page in the horrendously bloody history of the Catholic Church. One million people, probably a quarter of the population of France, was killed. At the siege of Béziers, Catholics were ordered to leave the city, leaving the Cathars behind, which they refused to do. The whole population of 20,000 was exterminated. All in the name of the God of Love. And must we remind of the war waged by the Church against *women,* condemning tens (maybe hundreds) of thousands of them to the most atrocious death possible, by burning alive, on accusations of supposed witchcraft?

Nor were the Jews intrinsically separate from and above the spirit of the times and places in which they lived. The early Church forbade marriage between Jews and Christians, but so did Rabbinical law. As bright a light of the spirit as the Jewish physician and philosopher Maimonides, contemporary of the most gentle St. Francis, pronounced that Gentiles were not to be killed, but should not be helped or saved. For instance, they should not be pushed into a well, but, should it so happen that they fell into one by themselves, they should not be saved from drowning. A Christian should be charged extra-high interest on a loan; and Christians should not be treated if they are sick. Or (the same Maimonides) that a Gentile woman who had experienced sex with a Jew, even against her own will, must be killed ("because through her a Jew has come to sin...") One would be hard put to find harsher commands in the pronouncements - if not in the actions - of Islam or of the Church. His list is long, some of it disgusting and terrifying. Fatal hostility came from both peoples. It is true that, when it came to action, the Gentiles almost always had the superior weapons of compulsion.

Dr Baruch Goldstein of Brooklyn (who must have taken the Hippocratic Oath to tend to all the sick) emigrated to Israel and treated Jews but refused to treat Arabs, then killed 29 Muslims with a machine gun in 1994, wounding 150, while they were praying at the Cave of the Patriarchs in Hebron, and was beaten to death following his act. He claimed to be a follower of Maimonides..

There probably does not exist a country in the world where some part of the population - be it defined according to criteria of religion, economy, occupation, geography, race, linguistics, or ethnicity - has not been persecuted, expelled, converted by force, or tentatively or effectively annihilated within any 300-year period. Not to mention the continuous repression of half of the world's population, women. *Sub species aeternitatis,* is there from the standpoint of the individual victim, who is the ultimate measure of a tragedy, some striking difference between the individual Carthaginians being wiped off the pages of history by the Romans and the million individual Armenians being massacred by the Turks? And the five or six million individual Jews put to death by the Nazis? Each person, each victim, takes his or her turn. And so does each Iraqi whose limbs strew the roadways of Baghdad. Each and everyone can be a one-person Shoah.

❖ ❖ ❖ ❖

Decisive help came to the aid of Zionism from Britain. Baron Walter Rothschild and Chaim Weizmann were both instrumental in its progress. Rothschild's financing was an imperative of the threatened British Empire in World War I. Weizmann had just invented a method of manufacturing cordite, which the German enemy had monopolized until now (and which produced a smokeless explosion). Their intense lobbying found its achievement in the Balfour Declaration of 1917, at first a classified statement of foreign policy by the British government. The British were then helping the Arabs to revolt against the Ottoman Empire and needed their friendship, as much or more than they needed the help of world Jewry and Zionism.

It ought to be noted that the text of the Balfour Declaration promises Britain's best endeavor to *facilitate* the establishment of *a national home* for the Jewish people. To *facilitate* means to help a project that others are carrying forward and a "home" is not a *state* and may simply be a privilege of liberal immigration or even a right to immigrate, although when the time came to renouncing its mandate, Britain could hardly enforce the immigration of Jews to Palestine. At another point, the draft of the letter had to be amended in order to make it clear that the "home" was to be *in* Palestine, not the whole of Palestine or a specific zone. On the other hand, the promise was serious, for it was officially incorporated in the Treaty of Sèvres with Turkey at the end of World War I., and in the League of Nations Mandate of Palestine conferred upon Britain.

But what hurt the Zionist reliance on the Declaration most are the highly specific lines: "it being clearly understood that nothing shall be done which may prejudice the civil and religious rights of existing non-Jewish communities in Palestine, or the rights and political status enjoyed by Jews in any other country." Both of these caveats had to be conveniently misunderstood by the Zionists when claiming the support of the Balfour Declaration.

Furthermore, it may be noted that these commitments not to prejudice the civil and religious rights of the non-Jewish population were added to the original draft on the urging of Edwin Samuel Montagu, a prominent anti-Zionist Jew who was Secretary of State for India; he was worried that, without these added lines, the Declaration would result in increased anti-Semitic persecution.

Always underlying Zionist pretensions was the conviction that the Arabs must go to make way for the oncoming Jews. Theodor Herzl himself believed so. "In his diary he wrote that land in Palestine was to be gently expropriated from the Palestinian Arabs and they were to be worked across the border "unbemerkt" (surreptitiously), e.g. by refusing them employment... Herzl's draft of a charter for a Jewish-Ottoman Land Company

(JOLC) gave the JOLC the right to obtain land in Palestine by giving its owners comparable land elsewhere in the Ottoman empire. According to Walid Khalidi this indicates Herzl's "bland assumption of the transfer of the Palestinian to make way for the immigrant colonist."(*Wikipedia,* "Theodor Herzl")

Still, before the coming of the Nazis, there was a different kind of Zionism, it seems. There was a real belief and dream about Jews who, if not returning to the soil of a land they thought they would love, at least would seek to make friends with the Palestinians and develop the mutual respect, understanding and collaboration that would culminate in a Near East Switzerland.

But the intensifying Nazi persecution, the growing anxiety and unfriendliness of Eastern Europe (until the beginning of WWII, Polish antisemitism was, for all purposes, as virulent, and affected a greater number of Jews than did the Nazi version), and the failure of the democracies of Western Europe and the United States to help the ever more hard-pressed Jews, turned the harassed people toward ever greater despair and hatred of both East and West.

The wide-eyed, "good-guy" Zionists of Herzl's general persuasion became tough-guy Zionists, desperate to acquire a Homeland by whatever means were necessary. And their recruits

101

were more and more of this ilk, maddened by the scene that they had escaped from, yet compelled to watch it, without being able to help their situation. In these critical years of the changing psychology of the movement might have been born the gangster terrorism, with its deadly opposing factions, evolving rapidly into the crude structures of an independent state which practically blew the British out of the Mandate of Palestine and then devastated Palestinian society and its people.

.An already traumatized pair of hostile peoples – Jews and Arabs – was authorized each to take possession of an eccentric topography upon which each was to build a demarcated nation-state. Each component would govern itself under the general oversight ultimately of the United Nations. But from the official beginning, in 1948, and even before then, the Israeli and Palestinians entered upon irregular warfare that has persisted to this day.

Their struggle, which has involved from the beginning and intensely the United States, has kept the Near and Middle East in constant crisis. Politicians and experts from many countries have become involved and failed to alleviate conditions. The United Nations and World Court have tried on a hundred occasions between 1947 and 2008 to restore order to the area, but have failed.

Zionism and a Gaggle of Schemes

We remind ourselves now of the five formulas that have been tried or are being advocated, showing in each case an insufficiency, and sometimes downright evil. Whereupon we depict the sixth formula, the Fifty-first State, and proceed in the succeeding chapters to show how it would work, exhibiting a surprising simplicity, completeness and effectiveness.

Already alluded to is the first and most prominent formula, which is the actual one, the prolongation of the present bloody, costly attempt to parcel out two disputed sets of lands between two enemy peoples, who are to suffer interminably, or until some miracle of peace and accommodation should happen to descend. The Israeli government would in any case insist on retaining critical settlements of Jews, the Golan Heights that belong rightfully to Syria, and, one might almost say, any other properties or rights that would bring peace if they were given up.

Israel's chief founder, David Ben-Gurion, in 1937 wrote: "Erect a Jewish State at once, even if it is not the whole land... The rest will come in the course of time. It must come." (It came when Israel seized the balance in 1967, which ended the partition *de facto*.) The supervising power turned out to be the United States government, deeply prejudiced in favor of a Jewish State.

THE AMERICAN STATE OF CANAAN

Ehud Olmert, Prime Minister of Israel, said, returning from the Annapolis Conference of late November 2007: "If the "two-state solution" collapses, the State of Israel is finished."

If so, Israel should have finished as it began 60 years ago, for there never were two states. He meant that the roguish use of the two-state "solution" has served to fool the world that such a "solution" was going to happen, while everything was done to prevent it from happening. But if this trick finally were to stop fooling the naive people of the world, will Israel collapse or be forced into the two-state solution? Never the latter; so, fiction or reality, the two-state solution will not work. Nor will Israel collapse. Surely, it would take inordinate ineptitude on the side of the otherwise shrewd and determined Israeli governments, if a two-country solution were indeed their honestly strived-for goal, not to be able to impose it on a weak, captive and dependent population such as the Palestinians over six decades of supposedly tireless efforts.

The two peoples are mixed territorially already in Israel and in the West Bank and Golan Heights. To establish the UN stipulated boundaries of 1947 and further purify the partition would require moving two million people of both communities, aside from cutting into the problem of the Return of the Refugees. There live a couple of millions of Arab refugees each of whom has a claim to a spot of space where now likely rests an Israeli who has been assured that he has valid claims to the same spot. They would struggle endlessly for their claim. Most Israeli are now celebrating the sixtieth anniversary of a great land theft: some are hoping to stay fixed until the end of the world. Their most valid (in the sense of forceful) claim is that given by the god El - not yet Yahweh - and although Genesis specifies that the grantor was a man, and Hosea identifies him as an angel - to a man from then on to be called "Israel" in the dim beginnings of the Hebrew people. It is a tenuous fiction, but one has to tremble with fear at the threat of a great many people who make the delusionary claim, Jews to execute the claim and determined evangelical Christians to swear to their right to do so.

A second scheme would be to let the Israelis expel the Arabs who are clinging to Palestine, half of the total population of Palestinians, to go mingle somehow with the other half that sixty years ago was exiled in neighboring countries. Probably the felt or subconsciously demanded policy of the political and theocratic elite of Israel is just this. Thus the Israelis would enjoy an enlarged and mythically historical Greater Israel. This would, of course, involve six million Jews in Israel plus some five million active or passive helpers from Jews abroad in the ruination of

105

another five million Palestinians and incur for the Jews of the world the enmity of one or two billion people. Accordingly, at some point in time, as the Israeli government moves to a total "ethnic purging," this quasi-fascistic solution might bring on general warfare, with an Israeli-American slaughter-machine capable of destroying most of Arab civilization. Accidental inclusion and the American demand for "coalition" allies would probably spread the injury to other nations as well.

A third proposal would be to reduce the heavy aggressiveness of the Jewish side, wherever it is expressed, and to increase its fairness and tolerance, to the point of its acceptance by the Palestinians as the lesser of two evils, that is, "helotism,"or "serfdom" rather than "ethnic purging."

This would restore the land in its entirety, a State containing both Arabs and Jews, and laboring to adjust them to a life together. This good plan for a united nation was meant to prevail in the 1940's, when the British decided to give up their mandate. It failed because the United States government ceased to advocate it and went along with the Zionist idea of partition. Still, Palestinians would perhaps have become a pariah people at home and abroad, as once the Jews of the shtetl and ghetto were scientifically termed by the famed sociologist

Max Weber, peaceable, persecuted pray-sayers, occupied at low callings and heavily policed.

Could we not then be fast approaching a unique historical condition: a Palestinian pariah state within an Israeli pariah state? However, it may be guaranteed that the Palestinians would react to such restricted tolerance by seizing any occasion to revolt: there have been many occasions in history where an oppressed people is revolutionized in step with its ameliorated treatment. And the Palestinians have become a modern, educated people, ahead of most Muslims in their progress - and let us not forget that the Muslim world in general has progressed tremendously on the way to education. The number of university students in Iran, for instance, has progressed from less than 200,000 under the Shah to over 2,000,000 - more than half of them women. An institutionalized pariah status fir the Palestinians has long ceased to be an option.

By mid-2008, trends favoring a unitary state were increasing. Thus, 26 Palestinian intellectuals, aided by a grant from the European Union, calling themselves the Palestinian Strategy Study Group, issued a report on Palestinian options to end Israeli occupation. Try as they might, their avuncular advice could not guarantee measures that would allow a happy two-nation solution. So they suggested reverting to a United Nations

Trusteeship, or better yet, a single democratic nation where somehow Palestinians and Israelis would enjoy equal rights. The mouse who would bell the Israeli cat was not named, putatively the United States.

They did not have my book to help their discussions, nor for that matter did Richard Rosecrance and Erhud Elran of the Harvard Kennedy School, who published an article in the *Christian Science Monitor* suggesting that the two peoples might become a state of the European Union. I had already borached this idea in some passages hereunder, but found the American Statehood solution to be superior.

A fourth plan would reconstitute the Israel-Palestine population as two functionally distinct and orderly semi-sovereign governments, living harmoniously on the full territory of the two peoples. (I elaborated such a Functional Federalism on the Web at www.federated-israel-palestine-in-exile.org, for several years, with little public response.) This plan is not only possible, but generally acceptable, though somewhat complex and perilous. Its adoption would require much advance propaganda. It would probably demand that Israel be condemned and forced into the arrangement in the beginning by a coalition of nations and international organizations – armies, economic pressures, boycotts, held at the ready and definitely to be employed should Israel balk.

We need to remind you, unfortunately, of a fifth "solution." Some intellectuals and rogues talk of a "War of Civilizations," in which the aggression of a billion people destroys the societies of another billion people. The candidates for this clash would appear to be so-called Christians or Europeans against Muslims of Asia, Africa, and the South Seas. The former, with systems of mass murder and mass impoverishment many times more powerful than those possessed by the latter, would "win," if anyone can conceive of there being a winner of so horrible a contest. This idea seems to be in the back of the mind of many of the readers of (or those believing to have read) Professors Samuel Huntington and Zbigniew Brzezinski, it would appear, with the "neo-conservatives" coming out of the University of Chicago Political Science Department and Law School, such as Paul Wolfowitz, who strongly influenced foreign and military policy along with Donald Rumsfeld, and where the refugee Professor Leo Strauss taught his own brand of *Realpolitik*.

More congenial and contrasting are the Harvard and Chicago professors who enraged the Zionists and Israeli bleachers with a thorough study of pro-Israel lobbies, but did them little harm, since they presented no alternative that could save the day. They sounded an appropriate alarm, signaling for new anti-lobbying legislation, which American history has shown to be usually ineffectual.

The Sixth, and, we believe, the superior prospect, is to create and admit Israel-Palestine as the Fifty-first State of the United States of America. The idea first suggested itself to the author in a treatise on world government in 1968. It is preferable to all of the others. It is an offer that can't be refused.

Therefore we take up Plan 6: Statehood. The name of this 51st State, with good reason, would be Canaan.

CONSTITUTING AND ADMITTING NEW STATES

Several steps are to be taken in Palestine, Israel, and the USA in order to constitute a new land and government and bring it into the Union. There should be assembled a congeries of people and groups who will prepare to ask for admission to the Union. Calling themselves the Canaan Statehood Movement, they need number only a few hundreds to begin with, but should include prominent leaders and well-respected citizens. They would submit a petition to Congress (both Senate and House of Representatives), and to the Israeli and Palestinian legislatures. From the beginning there should be launched a propaganda campaign to justify the new State. The Israeli petition should be joined to the Palestinian one, with practically the same wording. If both were to be submitted separately, Congressmen favoring the action could draft a Resolution offering Statehood, which would be referred to House and Senate Committees for consideration and reporting to the respective Chambers. Once approved, the bill would go to the President for signature.

Several processes would be happening at the same time:

* As the idea gains favor, a spearhead group might coalesce and structure itself formally and gather membership into a movement.
* A charismatic leader or the President of the USA might come forward.
* A simple favorable resultion might be passed through the Three legislatures involved to encourage the movement.
* Simple favorable resolutions might be passed through the three legislatures involved to encourage the movement
* A strong Canaan Statehood side should be elaborated on the Internet
* The general "Friends of the Canaan State" Movement military supporters where permitted, etc should beaccompanied in all countries and in the refugee camps and diaspora groups by favorable lobbies, trade union sections, professional associations, civil and.
* A Canaan Constitutional Commitee should becommissioned to draft an appropriate Constitution ofCanaan. Invitations will come to house the Committee in oneor

another legislature and in executive departments, but it may be preferable to convene the CCC at the headquarters of the Council of State Governments (in Lexington, Kentucky).

* If a public opinion survey were to indicate a substantial support for Canaan Statehood, presidential candidates would be inclined to take up the cause. A mere declaration that the idea is worthy of serious consideration would shake the public forum like a mild earthquake of 5.5 on the Richter scale.

* Such events would persuade a Canaan StatehoodTeam of some Israel and Palestine legislators to introduce simple resolutions encouraging a movement to investigate and report back on Statehood.

* Meanwhile the Team would hold public meetings in all sectors of Israel and Palestine (including refugee camps and world metropolitan centers like Paris and London) to explainthe Canaan Movement and bring in supporters and volunteers to convey the Plan around the world and into all parts of the USA especially, so that the whole world knows what is happening.

* Peaceful demonstrations are held where permissible, but never where disorder might occur.

* Canaan State USA is incorporated as a non-profit organization. Any established political party may adopt Statehood as one item of its program of demands, but no Party can claim the idea or the movement exclusively. Hopefully most parties in the legislatures of the USA, Israel and Palestine will adopt and work for Statehood.

* A special Team might be formed out of the movement, that would liaison with all State governments of the USA, seeking their approval to have the State of Canaan join the Union.

* A special Team might be formed to liaison with the Arab states and Turkey, especially those neighboring on the boundaries of Israel-Palestine, the future Canaan State.

* Teams may organize for Statehood both in Israel-Palestine and in the USA , also with the United Nations and with selected Non-governmental Organizations (NGO's) and also around the world (in the name of peace and humanity).

* Professional groups, such as trade unions and academic and scientific associations can resolve for Statehood, form Teams, and petition Congress to act.

* Several Israeli and Palestinian groups exist, such as *Gush Shalom,* that might

cooperatively propose and agitate in every way possible for Statehood. They must first of all be converted to Statehood.

* With the support of *Canaan State, USA,* an independent, peaceful citizen's union of Israel, upon consultation with its government, might suggest to a parallel group of Palestinians that they, too, form, and consult with their governments, putting forward in each case the numerous advantages to be achieved by Statehood.

* Canaan State, USA should welcome the approval of all Zionist, Islamic, Christian, Judaic, and other sectarian groups but beware of losing any of its complete freedom to seek exclusively Statehood for Israel-Palestine, which of course is now to become a well-guarded secular government.

* In any event, the guiding Team should be composed both of Israelis and Palestinians, with an associated American group.

* The Canaan 51st State Movement should as soon as possible seek out legislative representatives who would introduce the proper Statehood Resolutions in the three jurisdictions concerned.

* The Canaan Statehood Movement might consider a Steering Committee with a

Secretariat. It might include two each of Senators, Congressmen, Knesset legislators, Palestinian legislators, the Council of State Governments (USA), and 3 members of the Guiding Team of the Movement (A Chairman of the Committee, a principal Administrator of the Secretariat, a Chief Liaison Officer).

* As soon as a pamphlet describing the Statehood Movement has been widely distributed, the Secretariat should conduct a) a scientific sample survey and if approval is evident b) ask for a second larger confirming scientific sample survey in lieu of a popular referendum on Statehood. The survey would include people over 16 years of age of the State of Israel, the Components of the Palestinian Authority, and every Palestinian Refugee Camp. A sample of Israelis and Palestinians abroad elsewhere in the world might also be reached. All survey votes from all parts of the proposed State of Canaan would be merged and counted together and if a majority favors Statehood, this public approval would be forwarded and submitted by the Secretariat to the Speaker of the House of Representatives for

submission in support of a Joint Resolution of the two houses of Congress.
* Meanwhile the Steering Committee will have drawn up the proposed Constitution and performed an unofficial canvass of the opinions of all the members of the three legislatures concerned. If approval is forthcoming from the full membership canvass, votes taken in the Israel and Palestine legislatures, and the public opinion surveys, the Steering Committee should present both the proposed Constitution of Canaan and supporting materials to the Speaker of the House of Representatives who would arrange for Congress to vote on the Resolution of Admission of Canaan to the USA.

If the Constitution, with any amendments, is approved by Congress, and by Presidential signature, and a subsequent popular referendum in Canaan confirms its accord with Congress, Canaan is declared the 51st State on the date of this vote, with the right to elect at the proximate federal elections its two Senators and allotted Members of the House of Representatives (around 15 of them as its percentage of the whole population).
The Speaker of the House and the Majority Leader of the Senate might each name three Members of

117

their Chamber to constitute a Joint Canaan
Statehood Adjutant Committee to assist the
transition of Canaan into a fully functioning 51st
State.

Once a State, always a State. Canaan is not allowed
to secede. Prof. William C. Mullen of Bard College
has raised with me the question whether, because
of some disaster, if a large terrorist movement arose
in Canaan or other States, Congress might not
expel Canaan from the Union. This would be
unconstitutional and unadvisable in any event. The
conditions of getting Statehood in the first place
would make this scenario quite unlikely.

❖ ❖ ❖ ❖

Canaan's Constitution would be typical in
most regards of State Constitutions. It would
probably begin with a preamble declaring its intent
to provide its citizens with general powers, rights,
and welfare. It would include a bill of rights,
contain the same rights in various sections, in line
with the Federal Constitution, as amended. It might
also include some right that is appropriate but was
not thought of or considered necessary by the
Federal government. The State, after all, has a wide
range of independent law-making powers. For

instance, historically, the right of women to vote could be found in various State constitutions before it achieved a universal application in the Federal Constitution.

The Canaan Constitution would specify certain aspects of the right to vote, the officers to be selected, how and when, with their functions and duties, and, depending on how they are counted, hundreds of local governments and administrative districts.

Generally the Democratic and Republican parties monopolize the vote cast for important offices. Occasionally a third party or an independent group will move into the election process and win elections. With two parties, the electorate tends to divide rather closely and this fact in turn forces the party positions on issues to be close, rather than radically different. The heavy support given to their own State parties by the two national parties cannot generally be matched by impoverished independent State parties.

No doubt, the Canaan State constitution will be typical in most regards of State systems. A few minutes research into the many sources comparing State and local governments will indicate all activities of the States, and from these one can choose safely, and one may also propose an invention that can be tested against the US Constitution and the huge volume of court cases of

119

the hundreds of Federal and State courts. (Digital comparisons and analyses are ever more helpful and commonly available.) Numerous methods of arranging all kinds of State and local offices, functions, taxation finances, education and so on offer themselves for exotic demands to be made by the conjoined Israelis and Palestinians.

The US Constitution will not tolerate religious sects as such holding a right to public office. It will not let a religious sect's ministrations be required for marriage nor demand religious compatibility in a couple to be married. Still, the shadow of religious beliefs hangs over American lawmaking. For instance, a State can make divorce difficult or simple, and this has to do with the power and pressure of those religious sects that disallow divorce as a violation of sacred vows. It can control abortions, possession and use of weapons, widely varying schedules of punishments for crimes, and many other forms of behavior. It devises its own tax systems, though it must accept the federal system as well, and sets its own tax rates.

Jerusalem, considered a sacred center of religious activity by Christians, Muslims, and Jews, presents serious problems presently. It is a tinder box of fiery beliefs. It is also an ordinary city, if one ignores the sacred aspect, and presents fewer operational problems basically than a busy, highly mechanized American city like Newark, New

Jersey, or Houston, Texas, with giant airports and fleets of giant trucks moving day and night, not to mention the erratic behavior of its citizenry.

It would be a mistake to give it special status defined in terms of a species of Judaism, Christianity or Islam, or any other religious sect. The Vatican City is the State of the Roman Catholic Church; it used to be much larger, comparable in territory to Israel-Palestine. But it was occupied by the Italian Government in 1870 and the ensuing controversy was not resolved until the Lateran Pact of 11 February 1929 which left it with about half of a square kilometer of land but a guarantee of sovereignty. Its government is called the Holy See and is recognized worldwide, with the powers and functions of an ordinary state and membership in most international organizations. Under Canaan, Jerusalem would not at all resemble the Vatican.

In the event of Statehood, nothing would prevent Jews and Arabs and any other religious or lawful secular groups from associating with any religious or lawful organization in the world. Further, they might maintain their headquarters in Jerusalem, Canaan, USA. Disputes as to properties and rights of usage would be settled as similar problems are now handled under the State and Federal Constitutions. Some cases at law are likely to be interminable, but so long as violence, usurpation, trespassing and vandalism are prevented, there need be no special concern over the effects of Statehood on Jerusalem.

Furthermore, and this shall be the focus of our next chapters, the State of Canaan will have to go over its existing laws and practices with a fine-tooth comb to rid them of inconsistencies and violations of the Federal Constitution law and practices. The government of Israel has rung up sixty years of activities that are undesirable and unconstitutional according to the US Constitution and to what we hope will be the improved requirements of the Canaan State Constitution.

The government of Palestine comes under a lesser panoply of misconduct. Its accidents, its misfortunes, its few achievements have been limited to bare survival. Still, their rogueries, to be dealt with below, need to be eradicated or guaranteed of eradication as well, before the Palestinians can join the Israelis in offering a Constitution and civil conduct that are clearly and cleanly in order.

Finally, the time has come for a full functional reform of the American system of government. Middle East events of the past generation have observed the USA acting as a rogue state. Practically nothing it has achieved in this Near East part of the world is worthwhile or adds to a glorious national history.

❖ ❖ ❖ ❖

Several American Colonies met in 1754 and proposed what has been called the Albany Plan of Union. It was a defensive alliance, a way of dealing with Indian nations and a division of various mutual costs. A Confederation came about after the Revolutionary War (1781-88) and called itself "a Perpetual Union," but it lacked an independent executive and judiciary and was like a treaty of alliance - it could only get its moneys from the States, not by its own taxes. It had no troops, and could not regulate commerce among States. Amendment to the Articles of Confederation had to be approved by all 13 constituent States.

By 1785, a set of prominent leaders, North and South, were ready to agitate for a more national and sovereign government. After the famous Convention in Philadelphia of 1787, its product was put through the process of ratification. The draft Constitution was sent to the Congress of the Confederation which approved it, despite its exceeding by far the powers granted the existing Confederation. The proposed Document was then sent to the State legislatures, who were instructed to call special ratifying conventions, and the electorates of each State voted for delegates to the conventions. After a great deal of hassling between

123

Federalists and Anti-Federalists, the Constitution was approved by the minimum necessary of States and later by all 13.

But Massachusetts insisted upon adding a Bill of Rights which consisted of 10 amendments and these were to be voted upon once the government was in operation. They were so approved December 15, 1791, and correspond well to the Human Rights provisions of the charter of the United Nations. These are by no means the sole guarantees of rights. There have been 24 Amendments to the Constitution. One gives the vote to women: we have noted that several States had already done so, but in 1920 the Federal Constitutional Amendment made the right obligatory upon all States. Later, the age of voting for all otherwise qualified persons was set at 18 years of age; again, this was obligatory for all States.

Generally, the U.S. Constitution should be acceptable to most Canaans. (The *Constitution Annotated* is available on the Web and also with my comments in my book at <u>www.grazian-archive.com</u>. *The American Way of Government*, Part II, Chapter V.) At the same time, Canaans should appreciate that they will draft their State Constitution and can add rights, functions, institutions and procedures that appear useful to them even if quite original and unknown in other State constitutions, or in the Federal Constitution.

However, these novelties cannot be inconsistent with or supersede any provision of the Federal Constitution.

❖ ❖ ❖ ❖

Wars, massacres, and dissolutions of bonds between peoples have occurred thousands of times in world history. We have yet to invent a reliable system of peaceful relationships among nations or within a people. Probably no country has passed 300 years without suffering an internal or external war, severe persecutions, a split-up of group or territorial connections. In other words, every group is in perpetual danger of schismatics. Almost every cause of interpersonal conflict pops up every several generations at the least, on account of a marriage, a horse, a spit of land, a boat, an assassination, an insult, a bad business deal or begrudged treaty. The Arab-Jewish conflict ignited out of the embers of history which were blown into fire by religious fanatics and chauvinist desperados. Arabs sold land to Jews and then became bitter and riotous because they felt that they had nothing more to live for. Jews bought Arab lands believing that they would live in a rural dreamland with a God hovering above. But Israel became in short order a densely urban country, hardly one of

125

Biblical rustics. Its citizens can scarcely contain themselves when there is a chance to go abroad or, in many cases, to move abroad.

On the other hand, those same citizens become incensed when some Australian Jews offer help to Jews from the Republic of South Africa who may want to immigrate to Australia to evade violence and a people to whom they cannot well relate.

I foresee no end to the irritability of the Jews of Israel until they feel free to go and come in the wide world. Half a million Jews live in Los Angeles surrounded by and mingling with millions of fellow-citizens of every race, religion, and life-style. It is an absurdity to live and die by the claim that to live alongside Arabs is impossible. And the same absurdity applies to Arabs. We recognize that it is hard to get rid of the animosity and civil conflict so long as each group has, let us guess, some 10% of determined destroyers of the peace among them. But this is precisely why the Canaan solution will work. This 10% on either side will come up against a total population that is no longer terrorized or tempted by them. The 10% will begin to feel the comforts of ordinary civil law and the foolishness of shooting at phantoms. Can they any longer feel humiliated if they are American citizens? And what about the nightmares of ethnic purging? They may disappear overnight.

❖❖❖❖

American voters have several ways of electing their representatives to their State legislatures. All States are bicameral, but there would probably be no constitutional objection to Canaan experimenting with a single-chambered legislature. This author believes a single State Assembly can do the job well without a Senate. But, if conventionally bicameral, the State would be cut up into senatorial districts (say 100 of them) and assembly districts (say 200 of these). The districts should be of equal numbers of people (for instance dividing a State population of 10 million by 100 giving 100,000 people within each senatorial district. And the districts should be compact like chessboard squares as far as possible. Most States simply allow a citizen living in the State to get on the ballot by finding a number of voters who will sign a petition to put him there. Usually only the Democratic and the Republican Party candidate have a chance to win, so third or fourth candidates are discouraged from running for the office. The candidate with the plurality of votes (usually a majority) is elected. A great many units of government subtending from the State government are also headed by elected officers; they include

127

county, city, township, and special districts charged with such matters as conservation, water supply, education, and taxation.

At the top of the ballot one finds candidates running for Governor, Lieutenant-Governor, and usually several other officers such as a Secretary of State, a State Treasurer, a Board of Education, and more. The Canaans drafting the Constitution might as well follow in as many regards as possible an existing Constitution of a State that is similar in size, population, and principal industries. Creativity and invention in the design of institutions are in short supply, but a State can experiment with some new idea if it feels some special problem requires special treatment.

Special types of elections are used for calling constitutional conventions, amending constitutions, recalling elective officers who are disliked, and initiating or amending laws.

The Knesset employs the List System of election which moves away from the majority system used practically everywhere in America to a system of proportional representation where each party is accorded seats in a legislature in proportion to its vote total, more or less. Palestinians are familiar with it, and it is of course, the common method of election used in Europe (but not the UK and generally not in France).

Professors of American Government hardly teach of elections beyond the simple majority (plurality) vote system choosing the most popular of two or more candidates. They also teach that a second election of the two front runners, a runoff election, can he held soon afterwards if there are more than two candidates and no candidate gains a majority. They disparage the various systems of voting and counting votes preferred by most European countries, such as the List System that divides the nation into a number of districts usually of equal population and assigns a certain number of candidates to be elected from the district.

Under the List System, parties put up their favorite candidates. And the Party list gets as many of its candidates elected as the quota divides into the total vote earned. So if a popular screen star or philosophy professor or both head the list of the, say, Socialist Party, voters vote more heavily for the party and every candidate on the list profits.

In the end count, each party gets as many seats in the legislature as its vote reaches a quota. If 40% vote socialist and there are ten seats in the district and 40,000 people happen to qualify and do vote, it will take 4001 votes to win a seat, and the Socialist list will elect 4 candidates of the ten to be chosen, the 4 at the top of the list. Other parties divide similarly the remaining 6 seats. (To repeat:

by placing popular figures at the head of their voting lists, parties can irrelevantly or naughtily enhance their vote total and carry in humdrum candidates.)

We ask two questions: is this system – rather like that of Israel today – (we do the same for the Palestinian voters) permissible under the US Constitution? If so, it may and will be used as long as the Canaans wish to go along with it for the election of their 15 members of the US House of Representatives.

Thus 8,000,000 Canaans (seats allotted would be the number of seats in toto (435) divided into the 300,000,000 Number of Americans) would allow Canaan 15 seats. With 40%, the Socialists of Canaan would win 4 seats, the top four men or women on their list, let's say: the Party boss, a movie star, a wealthy woman and a terrific young orator??

The US Constitution will permit this and other proportional elections system, unless the Supreme Court becomes ever more conservative.

But the experience of Israel thus far and of most countries using the list system is that it encourages several parties to exist and therefore, afterwards, makes it more difficult to organize the legislature, with shifting coalitions and with elections occurring at awkward intervals of time, and in back of each list a party boss unless he headed the list and was elected.

The US Constitution does not forbid Proportional Representation or a List System, such as Israel possesses. It demands a *republican* form of government. It forbids any tendency to establish a religion. (And here the Israeli courts and lawyers, out of some unfortunate experiences, will be alert to block intrusions of religious rites into law and government that are frequently proposed by the US religious rightists and evangelists.)

A new election system is quite acceptable if consonant with the Federal Constitution. There is, in fact, one large change in voting that could be made and would allow the Canaans to at least claim one distinct contribution to US government from the beginning. It might adopt the 'most favored candidate system' recently invented and propagated modestly by several US professors and scientists. Professor Stephen Brams, its co-inventor, sat across the hall from me at New York University. I gave him my old article on De Borda's Eighteenth Century system of ensuring a majority election and he gave me his article on the new system of ensuring that the least objectionable candidate (and usually the best liked candidate) will be elected.

This form of voting, better termed "Approval Voting," would probably work well in the 51st State. Any number of candidates may

131

present themselves on the ballot. The voter need only check the names of those candidates to whom he has no objection (even if he favors some even more). Each gets one vote. The total of a candidate's vote coming from all voters will be summed up. The candidate whom most voters would accept, would be elected. For example, candidate "Ibne Gerlack" may be one of 7 candidates for office. He is acceptable to and well-liked (or at least not disliked) by a large majority of Israelis and Palestinians - more so than any of the other 6 candidates. He will therefore be the winning candidate.

We must take note what a powerful incentive for this method of voting will be to reconcile Israeli and Palestinian voters, to put them on common ground. The candidate whom they least dislike and who has thus accumulated a large "favorable" vote will be elected.

The Governor elected at-large symbolizes the full State and is simultaneously possessed of the top policy-developing powers. He is also charged with liaison with the central federal government. The Canaan Constitution could adopt the unusual feature of letting the Governor appoint a Deputy Governor who will fill out his term should he decease, and will manage the State's operations for the most part, freeing the Governor for policy development and dealing with the legislature and Washington.

Let elections be held for the Representatives in year 1, the Governor in year 2 and the Senate in year 3 and let all revolve on a 3-4 year term.

The Judiciary should follow the US federal structure and also the Israeli (with a Supreme Court), with appointment by the President and 2/3 majority approval by the Representatives (this is so as to reduce partisanship in judicial appointments).

Canaan has been so torn apart over the past half-century that its election system needs at the very least a geometrical survey. Let simply the surveyors be turned loose to draw up districts of maximum compactness for, say, 130 representative seats and 30 senate seats. Every seat would contain about the same population. These would give us our State legislature.

Much trouble has beset America in districting for Congress. Here we have again a promising format: Canaan would have allotted to it, besides its 2 Senators, probably 15 Representatives, all, as we have urged, elected from equally populous districts. No prejudices should be permitted in the drawing of lines. Computers can do the job of assuring contiguity very well, given a ground map of the people's residences. Let the computer calculate such, so that there is a maximally compacted terrain occupied by each equal number of constituents.

❖ ❖ ❖ ❖

Religious convictions would by no means flee the political forums of Canaan USA. In fact, the question would be raised as to the role religion plays already in American politics where the fundamentalist, the Catholic, the Methodist, the Jewish, the Mormon voters eagerly seek out their own kind of candidate. Will not the Palestinians, numbering a clear majority of Canaan voters, elect the Governor, and clear majorities of the legislature and many local councils all over the State? If so, how could they use their marvelous new powers? To help Palestinians – as all immigrant groups, including the Jews, have used their voting power over the past centuries. But that is precisely what is needed and why Canaan exists in part.

However, moving from this primitive stage of political behavior to more subtle happenings, we see that it is not for nothing that Jews hold about four times the number of elective offices their proportion in the population would indicate. This is said without taking account of the even higher percentage of Jews in the political media and political management. Is all this talent going to ignore the huge Palestinian vote? Not at all. The talent will be doubly at the disposal of Palestinian politicians. For, not only will the professional readiness to serve a respectable client call them forth, but also in many cases they will be moved by the recognition of the needs of a large population that has been terribly deprived and has every need of the machinery of upward economic, educational, and social mobility. Furthermore, Canaan will draw a great many Americans of different ethnicity who will constitute a large swing vote and will respond to different issues.

I think back to how, in my own lifetime, the Florida political scene was changed from its Southern backwater constituencies by a heavy influx of Jews, Italians and Irish from the Northeast who remade the State, and then more recently the important political effect of the large immigration of exiled anti-Castro Cubans. Very soon the Israelis and Palestinians would divide themselves into Republicans and Democrats and begin, too, the practice of the balanced ticket: containing candidates of each group and a third for the Christians or humanists. Personal qualities, name recognition, and an issue of immediate importance would complement the party label.

The lessons for Canaan are several: there are various ways of structuring practically everything, none of them vastly important, although heated controversies attend most proposed changes. In a single day of work, a constitution drafting committee for Canaan could pluck from the shelf of the many typical schemes whatever is needed to fill out their constitution. Alexander Pope's saying is fully justified: "For forms of government let fools contest, what'er is best administered is best."

This means adding and appropriating competent honest and creative men and women to office. There is not the slightest chance that the Israeli and Palestinians who draw up their constitution will do less well than the typical drafters who have preceded them on earlier occasions. Nor is it likely that the character of the elective and executive officers emerging from the 51st State will be a whit less praiseworthy than the high average of the 50 States.

Canaan would find itself operating under a comfortable constitutional system. Once in the Union, it is guaranteed against being split up without its consent. Equality of constitutional right and power is the condition of all the States of the Union.

The Canaans would enjoy a rule of law, that is, an habitual resort to a familiar set of fair procedures for settling disputes between individuals and organizations. They would operate in a federal system whose central government had limited powers over their peoples and their own activities. The central government would work with a division of power among the executive, the legislative and the courts. They would observe that each of these also had ways or power to check excesses in the others.

They would in turn be sternly limited by the Constitution. For their own new Constitution would have to follow suit and in addition provide key guarantees, as for instance, guaranteeing free enterprise, due process of law, and equality of treatment to both their own citizens and all other Americans dwelling, working and visiting within their boundaries.

In addition to the checks and balances found in the three branches of government in the American States and Federal Government - executive, legislative and judicial, the federal system itself is vastly important in reinforcing individual rights. For it gives two sets of important offices, one federal, one state, having to follow the federal constitution. There are not only U.S. District

Attorneys who prosecute criminals, following up the FBI (Federal Bureau of Investigation), but also Canaan District Attorneys who prosecute criminals chased up by State or local police. If a terrorist escapes one net he may be caught in another, for example.

Canaans would have independent taxing and regulating powers while at the same time submitting to the central government's taxation and financial oversight. Their government would receive grants-in-aid to spend for purposes designated by the Congress and in many of their activities would occur in collaboration with federal officers.

❖ ❖ ❖ ❖

The States are quite uniform in their institutions: know one, know them all. Among the first State Constitutions drawn up after the first elections under the Constitution, the State of Pennsylvania provided for only a single house of representatives (defying the check-and-balance Senate idea). It abandoned it thereafter, to imitate the Federal and other State Constitutions. Politicians are rarely innovative: they "play it safe."

138

Not only copying each other, but copiously so, Constitutions have gotten longer with time, as I easily demonstrated in an article of the Council of State Government's journal by counting pages and putting their numbers on a scale of the years. Logically and politically awkward, the various sets of constitution-drafters, followed by a suspicious public that wanted everything spelled out, added whatever seemed to be a good piece of legislation. The already cumbersome legal systems redoubled their complexity and also the costs of an army of lawyers, clerks, and judges.

One might hope that our 51st State would contribute to an enlightened Union, by means of a brief exemplary statement of basic rules. Not much more would be needed – despite the general false belief that Jews and Palestinians cannot govern themselves without continuous debate and struggles.

In the final analysis, it is the consistency, integrity, and efficiency of the courts of law that brings justice and guarantees the spirit of the law. Israel and Palestine have struggled without great success to bring about a rule of law. Unfortunately, the US system is imperfect, too: but this situation may present an opportunity for all-over improvement in the 51 States. For the tradition and honor of Jewish law are high and only need to be revived, by the one new State seeking enthusiastically to demonstrate how it could be first among equals in impeccability. For this very thing happened to the sprawling and incoherent American courts and justice when, after a long period of un-exemplary practice, a period of sharp improvement set in, led by Jewish lawyers and the merging of Jews, no longer discriminated against, in significant part into the profession.

Too, Israeli and Palestinian justice will be challenged and eager to work miracles, after suffering from gross political and ethnic perturbations. It has been the practice in American jurisdictions, when court dockets become crowded, to borrow judges from less occupied courtrooms. This could be done on a large scale in Canaan where a huge number of cases will need to be disposed of. Judges could be borrowed from States around the Union. There would also be a temporary shortage of judges, lawyers, and prosecutors who know American law and procedures. A flood of lawyers would be seeking licenses to practice law in Canaan.

At the same time pressures would be heavy to re-educate Israeli and Palestinian lawyers to American law and procedures. We may confidently predict that Yeshiva University's Cardozo School of Law, whether in New York City or Haifa, will set up promptly a full curriculum to carry Canaan

CONSTITUTING AND ADMITTING NEW STATES
judges, lawyers and students into the American
legal system.

These and Canaan lawyers themselves
would be bringing pressures to bear on the Canaan
system to get it more quickly in line with American
State and Federal law generally. Here the
experience over a long time of the melding of
French-Roman Law of the State of Louisiana and
the Anglo-American so-called Common Law
would be instructive.

Since nothing need keep the Israelis and
Palestinians from voting on Statehood, they can
even now study and be taught American
government and society. In fact a volunteer
corporation, possibly funded by private citizens
and foundations, could arrange for American
Government teachers, of which there is a
multitude, to begin work as soon as possible in
Israel-Palestine. They would teach the prospective
citizens of the USA all that they need to know and
more. Considering how much enthusiasm would be
generated in this manner it would not be surprising
if, from the start, the new 51st State public would
attain the average level of civic knowledge or
higher.

❖ ❖ ❖ ❖

Several conditions for its acceptance must be satisfied by Canaan before Congress would invite it into the Union. Surely the Golan Heights must be returned to Syria at some stage of the proceedings. Seized in the brief War of 1967, they are regarded throughout the world as properly Syrian territory. Their population consists of a number of Syrian, Palestinian and Israeli settlements. All but the Syrians must be repatriated to Canaan or elsewhere in the United States. This action alone would be most welcome in Syria and throughout the world. At the same time, the USA and Syria might well determine to demilitarize the frontier region.

Adjustments of a minor nature are past due also at the Southern border region of Lebanon, where Israel has been holding territory illegally. And, once again, the frontier should be demilitarized. In fact, while we are it, it would be sensible to draw up a treaty that would embrace the USA, Syria, Iraq, Lebanon, Jordan, and Egypt, so that there would be a demilitarized zone all around Canaan.

In this case, separate agreements might be made with Jordan, Lebanon, and Syria to return the Palestinians to Canaan, USA. If, as is likely, a couple of years are required to accomplish the Return, Canaan (USA) can agree to sustain the costs of the refugee camps until they are vacated. Canaan would issue bonds covering the costs of the whole Return Program on the world security market, with Arab nations prominent among the lenders, out of amity, and at low interest rates.

There would be concern naturally as the Statehood process looms up that millions of new US citizens would have to be provided with a place to live and means of livelihood. The simplest way to manage this is to create, immediately following the granting of Statehood, a Council for Physical Reconstruction of the best architects, builders and social planners in the world for drawing up a master plan for the reconstruction of Canaan. The whole job could be done in four years. One has precedents in America (such as shipping millions of men and all the foodstuffs and armament required across the ocean in 2 years), or in some of the mind-boggling feats of mass construction and population movements managed by the Chinese government in years past. I make note of the convenience involved in this operation whereby a million avid unemployed workers would be immediately made available for the immense reconstruction.

A second Return Program can raise the funds required, make the plans for, and reconstruct the large areas of Canaan that need to provide dwellings, community facilities, and workshops for several millions of persons who will be entering upon new homes. Here the International Monetary Fund, the World Bank, and the U.S. Treasury should put together the consortium to finance the Return Program. About $15 billion dollars for each of the two programs should suffice, allowing $10,000.00 per capita for the 3,000,000 persons we estimate would be directly provided for, and providing a sufficiency therein to cover most of the improvements needed by the population as a whole.

❖ ❖ ❖ ❖

A final paragraph here will summarize the admission procedure. Promptly upon the determination by the Palestine Authority that it wished to join with Israel in becoming the State of Canaan, the state of Israel and the USA would recognize the state of Palestine. On the same day, in the same room, and with the same pens, representatives of the three countries would a) recognize each other as nation-states; b) would

144

agree that the nation-states of Israel and Palestine should unite in a single State henceforth c) be invited by the United States executive branch to become a territory of the United States and d) to accept an outstanding offer by the Congress of the United States to become a 51st State known as Canaan. As I say, all four of these documents would be signed in quick succession at the same meeting of the same day and at the end of the day, America would have its 51st State of Canaan. Precedents for part and all of this set of actions exist. But never the totality and the universal importance. It would be a highlight of the Century.

The cost of having a beautiful sacred land is a small fraction of what warfare and defense preparations have cost the three nations involved in the creation of Canaan. I feel that Canaan would become within twenty years one of the best governed of the United States of America.

THE MEDIA AND EDUCATION

Jewish teachers have not surrendered their fortresses to the State of Israel. I revert to a study by Yohanan Manor, Chairman, the *Centre for Monitoring the Impact of Peace,* on 500 Israeli school textbooks of 1999 to 2002 on all 12 grades of all social studies disciplines. There has been a radical change in their content from the 50's (when the old aggressive Zionist outlook dominated), and the 70's, where the Arabs began to assume human shape.

The three periods of civic education in the Israeli schools, as discovered by Professor Bar-Tar of Tel-Aviv University and Prof. Eli Podeh of the Hebrew University of Jerusalem, are described by Prof. Manor: <http:www.edume.org>

> "Professor Bar-Tal, of the Department of Education of Tel-Aviv University, has noted that societies involved in intractable conflicts develop appropriate psychological conditions

which enable them to cope successfully with this kind of protracted and irreconcilable conflict situation. Bar-Tal mentions several "societal beliefs" which are instilled through the educational system and are conducive to the development of these psychological conditions, among them: "the justness of one's goal", "the opponent's de-legitimization", "positive self-image" and "victimization".

His conclusion is that the analysis of the school textbooks for language, history, geography and civics recommended by the Ministry of Education in 1994, "showed that the content of the textbooks used in the 90s differed dramatically from those used in the 50s and the 70s. The emphasis on the societal beliefs whose function was coping with intractable conflict decreased considerably. Only a small part of the school textbooks focused on societal beliefs concerning security, positive self-image and the victimization of Jews. The de-legitimization of Arabs almost disappeared, but their negative stereotyping still continued. Some textbooks attempted even to transmit new societal beliefs which promoted the peace process and coexistence with the Arabs.

He goes on:

"Eli Podeh, Professor of Oriental Studies at the Hebrew University of Jerusalem, has also pointed out that since the middle of the 80s there has been a radical change in the presentation of the Arab-Israeli conflict in the Israeli textbooks for history and civics. His diagnosis is even more clear-cut than Bar-Tal's, since he does not have his reservations regarding the maintaining of negative stereotyping. Podeh distinguishes three periods in the history of the Israeli textbooks: the childhood period (1948-1967), the adolescent (1967-1985) and from 1985 the adult, during which the radical change occurred.

"During the "childhood period", the educational system focused upon instilling Zionist values. The historical narrative was "simplistic, one-sided and often blatantly distorted" (p. 76). The textbooks of this period were clearly "filled with bias and stereotypical descriptions", as well as with errors, misrepresentations and deliberate omissions. "Arab history, culture and language...were almost completely ignored". (p. 74) "Savage", "sly", "cheat", "thief", "robbers", "provocateurs" and "terrorists" were typical adjectives when describing Arabs. Their actions against the Jews were dubbed "riots" and "pogroms" or "the events" and their perpetrators labeled "bandits". "Any information that might have marred Israel's image or raised doubts about the Jewish right about the land of Israel was instinctively omitted" (p. 76, *History & Memory,* op. cit.).

"The first seeds of change began to appear during the 'adolescent period'. The historical narrative was 'less biased and contained fewer (stereotyped) expressions'.. 'Moreover for the first time the Arabs were not treated as a monolithic group but divided into separate peoples, including the Arab Palestinian people'. The school textbooks of the second generation 'were not free of prejudice', but this was now expressed in a 'more sophisticated, and therefore perhaps more dangerous, manner than in the past. If previously the text alone was used to convey erroneous facts, slanted accounts and biased opinions, now maps, pictures, caricatures and diagrams reinforced this information. Furthermore sensitive issues such as the refugee problem or the 1967 war, were treated in much the same way as before: Israel was absolved of all responsibility or blame" (pp. 80-81, *History & Memory,* op. cit).

"But the watershed in the content of the Israeli school textbooks occurred during the 'adult' period, notably as a result of a directive, of February 1, 1984, sent out by the Director General of the Ministry of Education detailing the basic guidelines of an education program oriented towards "Jewish-Arab Co-existence".

There is a clear shift in the historical narrative, from a simplistic, unilateral and biased one to a far more objective and balanced one. 'Generally the Arabs are no longer described in stereotypical terms. Indeed, on the whole, these textbooks seem to present a balanced picture of the Arab-Israeli conflict. Even though it is still viewed primarily from a Zionist perspective, an attempt is made to understand the Arab point of view, especially in discussions of some of the sensitive issues in the history of the conflict. While none of the new textbooks is flawless, together they reveal the extent to which Israeli society and the educational system have progressed with respect to the way the Arab-Israeli conflict and the Arabs have been portrayed in Jewish textbooks" (p. 85 *History & Memory,* op. cit).

"In addition to the above-mentioned directive, Podeh pointed out two other factors to explain this drastic change in the content of the Israeli school textbooks. 'First, the appearance of a new historiography based on newly released archival material, which is more critical of Israel and the Zionist movement than before. ...Second, the improvements resulted from changes in the Israeli society with regard to the perception of the "other". Clearly, the changes in the history curriculum and in the content of the textbooks reflect a more mature society able to regard self-criticism not as a sign of weakness but rather as a source of strength.' (p. 61 *Arab-Israeli*, op. cit.)."

There is certainly bound to be a large improvement in Israel-Palestinian relations for which these courageous teachers deserve credit. And this will happily join together the Canaans as they approach their collective departure into the new Statehood. The Canaan Jews will be readier for a life as Americans. The revised textbooks and teaching that has led to greater compatibility between Arabs and Jews will by extension help both groups in their human relations with all other groups. And both Jews and Arabs need this outreach badly. Both have become misanthropes so far as the greater world is concerned. Both are misunderstood, too. Both have seen their reputations battered. Both need to become better world citizens, internationalists. Past and current Palestinian textbooks, it hardly needs saying, are heavily biased against Israel and need a corresponding reworking.

❖❖❖❖

Returning to consider the Jewish presence in world affairs, we need to distinguish the 'cosmopolitan' or 'globalist' and the more conscientiously involved 'internationalist.' The cosmopolitan is a man of the world at home in many cultures. A globalist is a person who believes that most human activities are more and more extensive geographically and culturally and that this trend should be used to advantage, personal, corporate, institutional and national. The internationalist seeks to add to the traits of the globalist and cosmopolitan a positive seeking for improved relationships in all regards possible among the individuals, groups and cultures of the world.

This is, of course, a logical distinction, and it is also demonstrable. Internationally active Jews have had to become tied to the USA, practically residents. Numerous newly wealthy Russian Jews have quickly connected with the USA, even though they have had to undergo unwelcome surveillance and compromises in their activities as a result.

Putting aside capitalist behavior, for the moment, we note that since the collapse of the Soviet Union and disintegration of international communism, the historically outstanding role of Jewish as propagators, initiators, defenders and spies of the communist lands has drastically declined. One perceives that Jews are no longer regarded as sincere helpers by those many Third-World non-communists who had hitherto possessed good feelings for communists because of the Third-World advocacy presented by the Soviet Union and other communist powers.

It is common for politically aware and active citizens of the Third World countries to project their resentment of US hypocrisy upon Israel. For example, while the US has been tolerating and even furthering Israel's armaments-overload, human rights abuses, nuclear explosives activity, and external aggression, while giving that nation disproportionate aid of several types, the US has also been sanctioning and criticizing and lending meager aid to the Republic of India with its billion people, mostly quite poor. The number merely of college graduates in India is several times the total population of Israel, and they are internationally aware, if not fully instructed.

One has to consider, too, the increasing elimination of Jews from the ruling elites of communist nations that was occurring in the decades prior to the collapse of most communist regimes. For example, Jews of the communist countries were received, protected and defended when they appeared in Third-World nations. The resistence to anti-Semitism was considerable. With the downfall of the Soviet Union and world communist parties attached to the Soviet line, and the prominence of the Israel-Palestine conflict, there was no longer this reason for Third World political activists and media to support Jews and, vice versa, Jewish globalists and Jewish causes generally tended to be rejected by them.

Moreover, accompanying the dissolution of the Soviet Union, as it attempted with its bureaucratic structure and hopeless incentives to compete in armaments and material production with the capitalist Western powers, was the shriveling of the socialist Trotskyite factions that were, for many Third-World and liberal, advanced-economy individuals, a way of sincerely advocating rights of Third-World peoples and minorities elsewhere in the world, against both capitalist and Soviet abuses. Whereas after World War II, Jews were prominent in the new communist governments, they lost this position gradually as enmity to Israel increased; old anti-Semitism surged in the Soviet Union and Eastern and Central Europe.

There is a balance, therefore, to be cast. Politically active and influential Jews have moved out of the political arena as international reformers in some large proportion in the capitalist world, but they have quit the communist world movements also, in some proportion. Communists and communist Jews were prominent among the anti-apartheid fighters of South Africa, at the time when Israel was one of the few nations of the world supporting the apartheid government. Given that liberal Jews who are engaged in agitation for world government and international brotherhood have declined in number, yet so have the Jews who are working toward a world that would be united under the banner of communism. Putting aside Soviet sympathizers, though literally acting as internationalizers, as good riddance, one would have to concede that, even so, a large loss in the number of internationalist non-communist Jews has occurred.

And this loss is all the more regrettable at a time when nationalist, junta, ultra-nationalist, sectarian, ethnic, apocalyptic and fundamentalist movements around the world are advancing. (Cf. *Le Monde* on the Web, November 21, 2001, an article by the leading Trotskyite theoretician, Daniel Ben Saïd, expresses unwittingly, but very well, the point being made here.) Consider the tragedy of Lebanon, in which this precariously balanced and productive center of multi-religious culture (including many Jews) was ripped apart because of its alliances, practically forced upon it by external and internal forces, and the violent reactions of Israel. Economically, socially, physically, and politically, the nation, instead of becoming a well-prepared partner of Israel, Turkey and Syria in the development and modernization of the Near and

155

Middle East, was culturally reduced by two generations of destruction and decadence.

❖ ❖ ❖ ❖

By eliciting a withdrawal of Jews from world concerns, the direction that Israeli government and society have taken since 1948 has been in part accountable for America's lack of progress toward world unity and brotherhood and to this grievous loss of advocates and activists among Jews must be added the depressed morale for world brotherhood and unity among Christians, secularists, and humanists generally. Seculars and humanists always drew much of their support from Jewish comrades. In the several years after World War II, the American movement for World Federation grew and flourished. It included supporters in the Congress. Senator Fulbright was one of them and introduced a favorable Resolution. Then the movement went into a long decline from which it has hardly begun to recover. The Cold War between the USA bloc and the Soviet bloc was the major factor in the downslide of support.

But note the interaction of forces: the new state of Israel was recognized and contended for by the USA and USSR, and became highly nationalistic in reflection of the world trend. This turn of events coincided with the cold war sentiments of American Jews, along with most other Americans. This author was active in politics in Illinois, California, New York, New Jersey, and Washington, D.C. and observed first-hand this trend. The deterioration of the "New Deal" agglomeration and prominence in the Democratic Party and the nation both contributed to and was caused by the aforesaid phenomenon. One could witness from the Seventies onward a shift of the more ambitious and alert Jews toward the "New Conservatism" (so-called), as developed for instance in "think-tanks" like the American Enterprise Institute for Public Policy Research of Washington, with which I collaborated on occasion over the years.

Rabbis of America and Israel run the gamut of credos and rites of Judaism. The average note sounded by American rabbis is more liberal and protestant than the average of Israel. Still one can expect in America, also, to encounter hopeful theocrats like the 33 rabbis who forbade a Jewish music festival scheduled at Madison Square Garden in March 2008, where the top singers of songs popular among Jews were to present themselves. Some rabbis went so far as to forbid any singing of songs written by non-Jews. Indeed there are rabbis who would forbid all singing. Madison Square

157

Garden is a gigantic version for true New Yorkers of the neighborhood saloon. The affair was cancelled and its sponsors lost 100,000 dollars.

This reminds me of a story told to me by my wife about her mother, who had a pretty voice and took singing lessons when young. This happened in France, just before WWII. At the French conservatory, the teen-age soprano had been learning songs in German out of the *Liederkreis,* a German romantic song-cycle by German composer Robert Schumann on poems by the German poet Heinrich Heine. The French being a civilized people, nobody dreamt of raising an objection. Then something happened that was unforeseen in the curriculum: the Germans invaded the country. In no time at all, the sixteen-year old girl and her teacher were told that it was forbidden from now on to sing these songs which she had been studying, because the words had been written by a Jew. The girl never returned to her singing lessons after that - not even out of protest, as she later explained, but because she took no pleasure in singing anymore.

The aforesaid rabbis are not alone among would-be theocrats and any US State where a religious denomination plays a role of any significance is likely to get its share of scoldings and threats of divine anger at spectacles deemed improper. Canaan will become outstanding as a

State where a theocracy had been hitherto attempted and in some part accomplished. Constitutional defenses of religious freedom would be put briskly to work if such religious tie-ins were essayed. They would not get far. A chain of State and federal courts stand ready to keep religious sects from dominating non-believers while ensuring freedom to continue worship by a variety of cults beyond that of any other country in the world. Canaan will become outstanding as a State where the very fact that Islam will face Judaism in large numbers will mean that there will be less likelihood that either one or the other can set the agenda for religious practice in the State. Both will receive the boon of tax forgiveness on contributions (which is really a contradiction of the First Amendment's injunction separating church and State, and lets billions of dollars fall into the collection boxes every year).

A lot of this money gets to Israel and I fear even out the muzzle of a gun, owing to the bad habit some executives have of mixing their monies. One of the ways the media have of favoring Jews over Arabs is in the picturing of Jews "just like us" and Arabs as contemptible. This resembles a Nazi trick I saw repeated a thousand times. The beautiful model Nazi - man woman or child - was seen posing smiling winningly "just like you and me would like our pictures taken," while the wretched downtrodden refugees, DPs, PWs, civilians and soldiers of Russian, French, Polish, Belgian, Greek, Italian, British, and Jewish ilk were shown "at their worst" in the eyes of the pain-avoiding, truth-avoiding public everywhere.

The situation acted upon even our own men, so that the wretched seemed hardly worth saving: we feel sympathy towards those we can identify with, few of us are not made uneasy by the sight of losers. Which these all were and therefore better to be ignored. Even upon conquering the Germans, the victorious troops would find themselves comparing the healthy, slightly disheveled foes with the ill-kempt abused crowd of aliens. This situation has prevailed with Jews and Palestinians in Israel and brings an unequal judgement, prejudices and treatment. There is a complicity of media around the world. Since its birth the state of Israel has enjoyed media support second to that given no movement whatsoever; no monarch, no religious cult, no giant corporation has matched the abundant sympathy and praise tendered it. Hundreds of eminent writers and politicians have sought in vain to bring negative criticism to bear upon the State. But the media voices favorable to Israel are overwhelming.

To the press, radio, movies, television and lecture platforms of the world, it would seem that Israel - a State given to many despicable activities -

could do no wrong. When an Israeli fell hurt or dead from a Palestinian stone, it bespoke a crime equal to the killing and wounding of a dozen Palestinians plus the destruction of their miserable homes. It is not only that a generous and humanitarian and civil rights establishment defends Jews vociferously against anti-Semitism and promotes their good deeds for the sake of what they believe is the Cause. Nor that a major segment of the media all over the world is owned and controlled by Jews. But, too, the media rely heavily upon consumer advertising revenue for their income, and Jewish activity in the retail industry is immense.

No one can have faith in the American media and many media abroad. Noone ought to believe the press, films, speeches, and propaganda. Nobody. The dirty job of the US and collaborative foreign mass media today is to cover up 95% of the Israeli government's offenses against justice, balanced news and comment, and people in Palestine. The high and mighty press and programmers bring down the 95% to 80%, and sleep soundly.

❖ ❖ ❖ ❖

THE AMERICAN STATE OF CANAAN

Build a greater Israel in the form of Canaan State, we say here. Dismantle Israel; if not, destroy it, say its enemies. Most Arabs say that it is hateful, evil, aggressive and foreign to the Near East. It is a mere neophyte to the real sacred soil of our times.

Why should Israel survive, then?

1. ? To assure that Jews survive, in preference to any one else. Thousands of tribes and peoples have extincted, including most of the tribes of the Hebrews.

2. ? To preserve the Hebrew language. Thousands of languages have died. Hebrew is a kind of Arabic without any great superiority. Israelis commonly speak Hebrew with an Ashkenazi accent, like Americans speak English with an American accent.

3. ? To preserve Jewish genetics. The Jews are a highly mixed group which to our mind is better than the unmixed. On average, they still show genetic relations to Arabs, signifying that Semitic is both a race and language far back and to a degree today.

4. ? To bring friends together more easily. A social club of people mirroring themselves. Togetherness?

5. ? To command the Middle East. Indulging the lust for power and overcoming Christian and Arab cultures?

6. ? To exemplify good government. Like now?

7. ? To bring forth a superior art. Music. Architecture. Fiction. Poetry. Science. Better than Jews have done in Diaspora?

8. ? To bear Jewish history in mind. What history? Familiar? More true history? The less it is worth emulating, the more to be avoided.

(8a) Jewry has a hundred wonderful histories in a hundred places around the world.

9. ? To eat better. No pork? No this, no that, and watch how you cook it?

10. ? To please god. Anthropomorphic religion. What god? What gods? Elohim? Mazda? Yahweh? Mars? Shiva? Baal? Jesus?

11. ? To move Jews into higher social and professional places. Prestiged universities? Prizes? Etc.

12. ? To not surrender to self-hate. Mutual reassurance.

13. ? Because other countries are even more obnoxious.

Conclusion: Israel SHOULD survive, as all groups beg for survival, because there have come into being all sorts of people and all these sorts of people share a collective belief that they should breed more people resembling themselves, a right which must be recognized to them by all the other people who make the same claims for their own, lest they undermine their own right to existence. Or, we may conclude that there is no more or less reason for Israel to survive than any other country, unless we can select from the above list of questions some positive affirmation of virtues that we share and wish to defend even at a high cost. The reader who can see through my pages will already know that MY reasons for existence are numbers *6, 7, and 8a.* As Thomas Jefferson said, "I am a religion of one." Not number 10, "to please God." One is tempted to quote Stendhal, "God's only excuse is that he doesn't exist."

Believing profoundly, then, in Israel's existence, we must know more about its mythology and propaganda, both such troublesome elements of political existence. Acting under cover of a mythicized history and the steered Holocaust (Shoah) memory, the effective governing group has committed acts that the internal opposition, with Jews elsewhere, and most Gentiles, might feel could be undermining the future of democracy in Israel.

By mythicized is meant strong beliefs in various Biblical, Talmudic stories, legends, distortions (such as the Massada "Last Stand"), and other events that are probably unhistorical yet serve to confirm a person in his resolve to build a greater Israel at any cost. Keith W. Whitelam, in his book,

The Invention of Ancient Israel, has discussed the process. Shlomo Sand, in: *How the Jewish People was Invented,* has followed suit.

For instance, the outside world has been led to believe that the Jews have been the ever-present major component of Palestine and Jerusalem. The Jewish population of Jerusalem and the region of Palestine has varied greatly in absolute numbers and in relation to other resident Palestinians. In a 14th century document only 70 Jewish households were recorded in Jerusalem while the non-Jewish population numbered 2,000 families. Opportunities abroad would diminish the number; so would hostile invaders of which there were many, none worse than the Christian Crusaders. Persecution abroad would send some Jews to Palestine and to other reception centers, such as Istanbul. Even today, after all that has been done to clear out Palestinians, the ancestral sources of the population of Jerusalem, crudely given to help their recall, are native-born Israelis, 20%; native-born Palestinians 20%, Soviet-born 20%, African and Asian-born 20% and the rest of the world 20%. Who belongs in Jerusalem? Who has a birthright there?

To take another case, the Shoah, or "Judeocide", as Arno Mayer termed it in his book, *La Solution finale dans l'Histoire,* La Découverte, 1990, are both superior terms to "Holocaust." (A

165

recent excellent brief account in French is by
Gerard Rabinovitch of the National Center for
Social Research in Paris, *Questions sur la Shoah,* and
see also Hannah Arendt's book on Auschwitz and
Jerusalem of several decades ago. The massive and
masterful account by Raul Hilberg, *The Destruction
of the European Jews,* and Norman Finklestein's book
on the Holocaust exploitation must be consulted,
as well as the latter's work on Palestinians.)

A loose meaning of the term Holocaust
allows most people to think of a large roasting fire.
This too is historically false and mythical, because
a great many Jews were killed by means other than
fire or died of hardships imposed upon them. The
Holocaust, in its original meaning, was a sacrifice
to YHWH, at which only the High Priest might
preside. An utterly solemn and dignified event. The
post-WWII version pictures the Jews, who were
put to death by various methods under the Nazi
rule in Europe during World War II, as being
burned to death in Great Fires, but a strict path to
the ancient rite would have the Jews as sacrificial
victims to the Jewish God (YHWH) and runs the
risk, in a logical analogy of the term, of making
Adolf Hitler, *Der Führer,* the High Priest himself, all
in one person.

The enormous judeocide was neither a
sacrifice nor a fire. It was extermination by the
most expedient means available to the Nazi

organizers, some of them developed for the mass murder of the German handicapped. Still, the Chief Orthodox Rabbi of Jerusalem (and others) has been so specific as to say that Hitler was sent by God to punish the Jews for a long series of offenses over time. Public outrage brought a weak recantation.

A large guilt comes into play here, for not having "done something" to prevent or stop the judeocide and other Nazi mass killings. These latter have been shunted aside in the popular mind by not being of comparable size, as if war prisoners - three million of them Russian - hundreds of thousands of Gypsies, and hundreds of thousands of partisans and political prisoners, helpless enemy or neutral troops, and falsely detained civilians need not be remembered, or, for that matter, as if any deliberate homicide does not fall upon its perpetrator with the same gravity. Readers of these pages can find an American soldier's view of the processes that marked the repression, indifference, psychological hang-ups and command decisions pertaining to the realization of the mass murders (based on correspondence and memoires but not published until 1982), in this author's *A Taste of War.*

Long after the war, I was lunching at a modest East Side restaurant in New York City with

Joel Carmichael, whose job in the war had been similar to mine, who had a project running at NYU under my supervision, and who edited a Zionist magazine, so good, in fact, that I was pleased to publish an article in it on Moses. At one moment, he pointed his knife surreptitiously at a man seated at a table across the room. "See him? He wanted to set up Hitler's assassination before the War, but could not arrange it with the others." A gush of regret filled my breast.

No doubt some Israeli propagandists would like to use the "Happy Niggers" ploy that Southern slave-holders once used to justify slavery. They cannot, because they simply cannot bar all communications to the Palestinians, although in 2002 they came close to it, burning and exploding whatever might be used for communicating, radio and television, roads, even bulldozing the car and wrecking the helicopter of the President of the Palestinian Authority. Then in 2007-8, they came close to shutting in and starving the 1.5 million people of the Gaza Strip.

Myth is used by the Israel government also in seizing and holding territory of other groups, and for denying property rights to Palestinians and other Jews. The principal myth has been shown to be false: the myth that the Palestinians voluntarily quit and fled, abandoning their land and houses. This was accompanied by the myth of the Empty

168

Spaces. Originally the Zionists were so ignorant of Palestine that they thought it was largely unoccupied and the land barren. (A Zionist fact-finding mission at the end of the 19th century did write back: "The bride is beautiful, unfortunately she is already married...") The belief, nurtured especially after the great Arab flight of 1948-9, has helped, as before, to persuade the world public that the Jews were moving into an underpopulated, even unpopulated, area. "Jest a few Indians, folks."

Myth lends itself to manipulation by propaganda. Both the Israelis and the Palestinians have exerted themselves to communicate their demands and expectations to the world in the best possible light. In this propaganda war, one encounters an immense superiority of Israel, in means and skills. The slogans commanded by the instrumentalities of Israel and its allies everywhere prevail: Holocaust; Promised Land; the Only Democracy in the Middle-East; the Terrorists who lead willing Muslim mobs; indeed a complete presentation of history and current events as a mind- numbing set of affirmations and defamations that have received a high polish and plausibility among the more "advanced" and well-to-do peoples of the world. Use of the term 'anti-Semite' in propaganda – one of the most devastating weapons, ranges from popgun accusations to severe campaigns of defamation, diffused or specific

The problem of Israel-Palestine gains its potency from a mystic religious sense, which should not be allowed to embrace and control political realities. Stripped of the need to kowtow to all of the icons and idols, the rituals and ruins, the solution in the Near East can be made into a solvable problem, more like assigning responsibility to two corporations, one vegetarian, the other carnivorous, to satisfy a set of needs of their clienteles. Without the heat of religious fundamentalism, it could be more like letting people choose one of two or more social clubs to which to belong, or becoming a Republican or Democrat in the United States.

Israel closed the schools and universities of Palestine so often and for so long that it is a wonder that Palestinians are still 92% literate. More than to put down rebellion in schools, it was the Israeli purpose to disperse the teachers, students, and learned institutions of the Occupied Territories. Praise the heros, those teachers and there were many Jews among them, who privately cared for and tutored many Palestinian children, often risking jail or gunfire for violating curfews, for congregating, for evading road-blocks. If ever the rogue state were to be refashioned, we might discover a generation of helpers and teachers has imparted a neighborliness, an altruism that could compensate for the hatred inculcated by the same destructive events.

Haaretz, the Israel newspaper, wrote recently: "In Silicone Valley they like to joke that there are three kinds of American entrepreneurs: Indians, Chinese and Israelis." Thousands of women and men of many countries and occupations have entered the illegally occupied lands of Palestine and become eyewitnesses to Israeli roguishness and crimes. Yet, "it is as if no one has seen anything." The impact of their testimony and corrective activity has been practically nil. The extent and intensity of Israeli destructiveness and repression has increased over the decades. So much for the openness and power of the press and grassroots public opinion. In relation to the moral and physical ruin visited upon the Palestinian land and people, the occasional bombs exploded by suicidal Palestinians have been a weak retaliation. The Palestinians have been commonly reduced to numbed desperation, the Israelis excited to conscious fear and trembling.

❖ ❖ ❖ ❖

THE AMERICAN STATE OF CANAAN

There is only occasional use in distinguishing education from propaganda. A lobby for instance both educates and propagandizes interrelatedly. A run-down of the list of activities of the American Israel Public Affairs Committee (AIPAC) reveals this fact in hundreds of ways. It is not old, formed in the 1950 by Sy Kenan, but here is its proudly publicized list of activities to which (need I add?) there should be appended thousands of confidential contacts and efforts within and beyond the named activities. AIPAC claims 65,000 individual members who must in turn contact directly or indirectly hundreds of others on numerous issues. All in all, a veritable army of lobbyists pressuring for favorable action at every porthole of government. Viz.:

I.   Two thousand meetings with members of Congress and 100 pro-Israel legislative initiatives a year.

II.   Activists work closely with AIPAC staff, people drawn from top echelons of government, diplomacy academia and politics.

III.   Policy experts review daily hundreds of speeches, journals and meet with innovative foreign policy thinkers.

IV.   Regional offices reach out to activists in hundreds of communities around the country.

V. A political leadership development program trains leaders in pro-Israel advocacy and students do all manner of political campaign work and liaison with other student groups.

VI. Scholarships are available for at least four annual policy and training seminars.

VII. The Schusterman Advocacy Institute gives special training in propaganda and political advocacy.

VIII. AIPAC works with Congress to stop Iran from acquiring nuclear weapons.

IX. AIPAC engages Congress to ensure the security of "the only democracy in the Middle East".

X. It seeks American support against the specter of nuclear, biological and chemical weapons delivered by long range missiles for which no defense yet exists.

XI. AIPAC is pushing for greater Jewish youth participation, whose Israel identification has been declining.

XII. AIPAC is working to isolate Hamas, Hezbollah, and Palestinian Islamic Jihad, and seeks a worldwide boycott of financial institutions that hold their assets.

XIII. Secures funds for Israel to purchase American robots and scanners designed to detect and neutralize bombs.

XIV   Pressures the Palestinian Authority to fight terrorism by urging sanctions if it does not do so.

XV   Seeks to stop US assistance to the Palestinian Broadcasting Corporation for its anti-Israel broadcasting.

XVI   Helps the US to develop defenses against ballistic missile threat and faster delivery of Arrow missiles to Israel and developing a tactical high energy laser against low flying rockets, also securing funding for weapons to destroy underground bunkers and securing funding to develop Israeli targeting system for improving accuracy of American air strikes.

XVII   Seeks to block foreign investment in Iranian oil and achieved overwhelming renewal of the Iran-Lybia sanctions act for 5 years.

XVIII   Seeks sanctions against foreign companies that ship missile technologies to Iran.

XIX   Presses the Russian government to end its weapons arrangement with Iran by getting the US to withhold aid needed by Russia.

XX   US provides and Israel passes along many millions in refugee assistance to absorb former Soviet Union immigrants.

XXI   Seeks special treatment in receiving assistance within 30 days after foreign aid bill is passed, instead of waiting for many months.

XXII   Educates law-makers and staff by arranging Congressional trips to Israel through its education foundation.

XXIII   Achieves resolutions by a 410 to 1 vote applauding Israel's recent democratic elections and restating US commitment to Israel security.

XXIV   Fights to have Jerusalem recognized as undivided capital of Israel on all US documents and maps.

XXV   Pressures to move US embassy from Tel-Aviv to Jerusalem.

XXVI   AIPAC works to secure Israel's acceptance into West European and other regional groups at the UN.

XXVII   Urges the USA to boycott the UN world conference against racism which spreads anti-Israel and anti-Semitic views.

XXVIII Seeks US sanctions against the International Committee for the Red Cross until it accepts Israel Mogen David Edom.

> *(All of the above items – none were left out – were quasi-copied in brief from a document provided by AIPAC on its home web site www.AIPAC.org)*

AIPAC, we need to point out, is but the grandest of pro-Israel lobbies of which there are hundreds. And a great many institutions are always ready to lend a hand - universities, companies, theatrical groups and all types of news media.

❖ ❖ ❖ ❖

When, for instance, Arun Ghandi, grandson of the liberator of India and also a pacifist, inscribed in a regular blog in the *Washington Post* remarks reproaching the Jews and Israel, an explosion of hostile public opinion struck him down. A few words of his may be quoted: "Jewish identity ... has been locked into the Holocaust experience... it is a very good example of how a community can overplay a historic experience to the point where it begins to repulse friends... it seems to me the Jews today not only want the Germans to feel guilty, but the whole world must regret what happened to the Jews. The world did feel sorry for the episode but when an individual or a nation refuses to forgive and move on, the regret turns into anger. The Jewish identity in the future appears bleak. Any nation that remains anchored to the past is unable to move ahead and, especially, a nation that believes that its survival can only be ensured by weapons and bombs... We have created a culture of violence (Israel and the Jews are the biggest players) and that Culture of Violence is eventually going to destroy humanity."

The parenthesis is inadmissible, because it is wrong, morally and factually (Americans are bigger players - aren't we?). And of course the whole world has an obligation to regret what happened to the Jews. Gandhi, with whom I had planned for a time, long ago, just after the Bhopal catastrophe, an organization for world peace and order, was excoriated by hundreds of letters, was forced to apologize as was the *Post*, also the University of Rochester where he had founded a Peace Institute, and he was fired from both jobs. So the President of Rochester, Joel Seligman, joined with the Presidents of other distinguished institutions such as DePaul University, Harvard University, the University of Chicago, and Columbia University in letting themselves be in a sense bullied, effects which are the more shameful for leaking out of the Higher Learning.

After former President Jimmy Carter published a book denouncing Israeli "apartheid," he found himself, despite his world-wide fame and Nobel peace prize singularly without invitations to address audiences on American television and with only bare coverage of his global activities in the press. When he went to Syria for conversations with the chief of Hamas, the government of Israel refused to see him. He was roundly abused at the United Nations by the Israeli Ambassador.

177

And Noam Chomsky, that resolute laborer in the vineyards of justice for Palestinians, makes no mention of Jews or Israelis in a book he co-authored with an Italian on the control of politics by media moguls around the world. Maybe he did not know it was censored. Maybe he could not read the Italian of his co-author. I should investigate this small matter.

If every suppression or deliberate distortion of a piece of disgraceful news attributable to party X by a medium of public expression is deemed a roguish act, then tens of thousands of such acts have served the Israel state over the past half-century. (Figuring a rate of one thousand per day emanating from all significant media outlets, estimated modestly at one thousand, of which 200 are newspapers, radio, and tv outlets, of the United States, 400 for Europe and 400 for all other countries.)

A favorite target of the media are Muslims as a whole, especially the Palestinians, and then Syria, Iraq, Iran, etc. One responsible well-done report in the *Christian Science Monitor* (www csmonitor.com/2006/1023/) asserts that American Muslims are fairly unaccessible to terrorist appeals, but interested rather in assimilation and acquiring typical American life-styles. American Muslims hold a consensus that recognition of a Palestinian State and of lending less support to Israel would diminish any world wide terrorist threat. There was a rise, hopefully temporary, in anti-Muslim prejudice following 9/11 among the American public. Most experts believe that the government's moves against terrorism have been exaggerated, and to that degree counterproductive, and also a great waste of money, representing a diversion from criminal investigation to antiterrorist measures.

I quote from this *Christian Monitor* study of American Muslims:

> "Most Muslim immigrants came to America for educational or business opportunities and from educated, middle-class families in their home countries, according to an analysis by Peter Skerry of Boston College and the Brookings Institution. In Europe, the majority came to work in factory jobs and often from poorer areas at home.

> "European Muslims today live primarily in isolated, low-income enclaves where opportunities for good jobs and a good education are limited. In the US, 95 percent of Muslim-Americans are high school graduates, according to "Muslims in the Public Square," a Zogby International survey in 2004. Almost 60 percent are college graduates, and Muslims are thriving economically around the country. Sixty-nine percent of adults make more than

$35,000 a year, and one-third earn more than $75,000, the survey showed.

"In Britain, by contrast, two-thirds of Muslims live in low-income households, according to British census data. Three-quarters of those households are overcrowded. British Muslims' jobless rate is 15 percent - three times higher than in the general population. For young Muslims between 16 and 24, the jobless rate is higher: 17.5 percent.

"The culture is qualitatively different [in the American Muslim community] from what we've seen from public information from Europe, and that actually says very positive things about our society," says Jonathan Winer, a terrorism expert in Washington. "We don't have large populations of immigrants with a generation sitting around semi-employed and deeply frustrated. That's a gigantic difference.' "

Cultural accommodation is readily possible for Canaan. Neither Jews nor Arabs have cultural stakes that are rare in the United States or incompatible with the ordinary routines of life. Santa Claus and the Crêche are about as much of a nuisance as the Israelis and Palestinians will have to put up with. They are already familiar with and often even enjoy these symbols and activities - the

Crêche, after all, hails from Bethlehem, in the West Bank; like every other special group, they will have to struggle if they want to escape the "Disney-embrace."

Nor can one readily call up Islamic and Jewish practices that are intolerable in the US, granting, of course, that they are not forced upon the secular and Christian majority. However, abominable rituals and public expressions are absent, or so private as to cause no open indignation.

Jews are intent upon and probably helped spark the idea of the nineteen sixties that America was not a melting pot, but groups of ethnics, multi-cultured. The melting pot had been the favorite myth and reality of America until then. It is possible that Jewish fundamentalists, in their fear of the disappearance of biblical Judaism, wanted to show that pluralism persisted, this tending to cultivate a double loyalty and to justify it by showing that Americans generally were ethnics, not assimilated. It is partly a matter of words, but the word *melt* means to disappear and *pluralism* means to maintain a cultural identity. And therefore the word *meld* which signifies the assimilation, but with recognizable differences shading off among groups, might work, where *melding pot* would be the preferred term.

THE AMERICAN STATE OF CANAAN

Both Israelis and Palestinians have stereotypes of Americans that are pro and con. It is common for Palestinians to believe that Americans are hopelessly misinformed people whose government and institutions behave hypocritically, that the media and government are controlled by Jews, that it is a comfortable and fair place for foreigners like themselves to live in and work.

Also, that an unfriendly fundamentalist Christianity prevails. Too, that America is an exploiter of Arab resources, yet also that America is an exploitable resource for Arabs, Muslims and Palestinians once they can get into it and connect up with it. And that it is an imperialist country that cultivates brutal regimes everywhere.

Among Israelis and Jews, generally, anti-American attitudes (that is, the government and population as it is imagined by many Israelis and for that matter the rest of the world) are alive as well as among other peoples. The US appears as a benevolent sympathizer and protector of Israel, but it is also Uncle Stupid. It needs instructions and watching. It is also Uncle Manipulable, exploitable in every way. It's people are mostly busy protecting their selfish interests. They are intrinsically anti-Semitic .

And, too, many Jews and Israelis wonder, "I don't love them, how could they love me?" They are a more distasteful, culturally more remote ally than the French or the Russians. They are bullies that may be dispensed with in dire emergencies, and they are Russophobic, Islamophobic and oil-grabbing.

Canaans and Palestinians would be concerned about competing with Americans. The Palestinians might welcome the fact that there are hundreds of thousands of black Muslims in America, but these Muslims would also be competing for their jobs, and of course the Israelis would excite the usual fear of out-competing the Gentiles.

❖ ❖ ❖ ❖

Various figures can be presented. 26% of reporters, editors and managers at the major media of print and broadcasting, 59% of writers, producers and directors of the top 50 receipt-grossing movies, the owner statistic follows suit but is difficult to calculate – one owns part or more, one owns one or more, one measures the weight owned by circulation and reputation by the example of how many media voices follow suit, copy, calm down, are indignant, are supportive, etc. in measuring influence. Take the top five newspapers, magazines, tv stations, book publishers, internet web sites, and movie production teams – the top and best, and at least one among their owners and highest officers will be Jewish. Which is as likely as it should be.

Unquestionably, an unbiased American journalist viewing the battle scene of Palestine could praise the Arabs for harassing the heavily armored Israeli troops as freedom fighters, as self-sacrificing, unpaid warriors with puny weapons, as tenacious despite heavy losses; but this reporter rarely gets into print, and would be unlikely to find permanent employment. He would do better to report the equivalent story of Spanish cannon against Indian arrows in the 16th century.

Teaching civics to Canaan youth is already beginning, as I indicate on another page. Remarkable progress has occurred in three phases of educating Israeli youth from the pre-state extreme Zionism, to a generally pejorative version of Palestinians and Arabs, to a fair-minded and conciliatory program for the two groups.

In America or France, as now in Israel, civics is ordinarily taught in the way Israel handles its courses, that is, by the definition of proper relationships. What would be asked further is practical education in getting along, living side by side, solving problems together. This is a difficult kind of teaching, and not at all accomplished in the advanced western countries either. Americans learn to meld by doing so, rather than by formal teaching, although the authority of the classroom backing up the melding is very important. Hot problems like the Palestinian Return, blockades of the economy, excessive force, social mixing, are so controversial that long and intense group work is needed and if it were properly and fully done in the schools, there would be little time left for the rest of the curriculum.

The positions of Jews in America have been shown to advance exponentially in the last century. There is not only the problem now of the Jews depending on the Gentiles for help in rising in social affairs, but the problem of the Gentiles being dependent upon the Jews. For example, in the media, gentile journalists must not only think of pleasing a gentile employer, if such is the case, but also think of the likelihood at some time or another of working for a Jewish-owned or managed newspaper or tv station. Further, if he is a professor he must think of the key positions held by Jews in the better universities. And the gentile who enters the acting profession or entertainment in general and the authors of fiction and non-fiction - all of these must consider that half the time they will be working in association with or under Jews. And of course politicians in constituencies where the

Jewish presence is heavy - but more than that, in all constituencies where Jewish lobbies are at work, which means everywhere – must tend to Jewish concerns with an above-average intensity. A few excellent studies of the operation of Jewish pro-Israel pressure groups exist. These pressure groups are so active and competent that they become name-registers of everyone who has expressed unfriendliness to Israel - never mind anti-Semitism. It becomes professionally foolish of any writer, actor, film-maker or professor to let escape words attributable to negative feelings against Israel.

Does this make for sincerity in the attitudes which are fostered in this way? Hardly, and certainly not always. Any set-back, any failure is likely to rouse anti-semitic feelings, unexpressed, and cumulating.

Israeli doctors have worked in Palestine in teams of several Jews and Arabs, going into villages and holding clinics. They have become comrades and then they have gone back to the usual cauldron of the Arabs and the more orderly Israel of the Jews. There are a number of other such cooperative groups which endeavor to ease the pain of existence in Palestine and the guilt felt by the Jews. The courage and sacrifice of voluntary groups of which *Gush Shalom* is outstanding, is hardly to be experienced in all of America.

❖ ❖ ❖ ❖

The greatest reservoir of possibilities for melding Canaan into America is the intelligentsia. The term intelligentsia favored by the Russian communists in the early days of bolshevism has never found an equal for describing the aggregate of characters and personalities that we have in mind. A member of the intelligentsia may be defined as a person whose combined knowledge, skills and decision-making are at the top 1% of the population. Thus, three million out of three hundred million Americans. But their number in their own group and the size of the group itself vary greatly. The large Century Club in New York is practically all intelligentsia of the literary and scientific world. The great International Brotherhood of Elks has many less in all its lodges than the Century Club. The scene is enormously complicated, rather like identifying, sorting and plotting the positions of bodies of the asteroid belt. The figures that follow are guesses concerning the top third of the three million, that is, one million persons, one out of every 100 adults..

Probably this American intelligentsia draws upon a "reserve intelligentsia," apprentices, rising youth, the retired, and workers capable of converting to intelligentsia work – not fully qualified, but presenting another million Americans.

Hereunder are the rough estimates, which can be challenged in part or whole, basted together by the author according to miscellaneous studies.

1	1,000	Leading politicians (not counting myriad local politicians)
2	10,000	Jurists (judges)
3	20,000	Media specialists
4	10,000	Catholics- clerics and lay persons
5	50,000	Protestants – clerics and lay persons
6	30,000	Jews (independent, while another 200,000 are counted in other categories) including rabbis
7	200	Palestinians
8	1,000	Muslims
9	1,000	Organized labor
10	1,000	State Department

11	5,000	Independent commissions and agencies such as NASA, SEC, FCC
12	3,000	Corporate network associations such as the National Association of Manufacturers
13	10,000	Informal "old buddy" nets, amateurs and clubs
14	10,000	Voluntary associations leaders
15	800,000	Professional associations (generally relevant such as educators, and directly involved such as the American Economic Association or the American Psychological Association)
16	10,000	Military
17	5,000	Mavericks: a)activists and agitators; b) rich and independent
18	10,000	Writers
19	10,000	Artists and actors
TOTAL	987,200*	

* Note: of the 987,200 probably about 230,000 are Jews of one type or another.

THE AMERICAN STATE OF CANAAN

To clarify in my own mind the process of estimating these figures, I had to resort to autobiography. As of June 10, 2008, I have numbered over 2000 acquaintances in my 90 years of organic (including in utero) existence and experience. Among them 40% would have been of the intelligentsia, because I have spent so many years at universities and on research projects. Given the average lifetime to my acquaintances of 70, possibly 100 are still alive, about one in twenty. Of these perhaps 60 are of the intelligentsia and 10 are in the top third of the intelligentsia. Of the ten, 4 are fully or partly of Jewish origins. Obviously, in old age one comes to depend more and more upon the media for intellectual nourishment. I must reach out for rare individual students or friends, or the media, to carry my messages. From the media must come also the messages of my friendly intelligentsia. That is why Marshall McCluhan was *so* clever when he said long ago, "The medium is the message."

GARRISON STATES

The garrison state is a concept invented by a leading American political scientist, Harold D. Lasswell, in the early 1950s, during the period of so-called McCarthyism. That was a quainter persecutory period than the present, in that it was concentrating mainly upon entertainers, the left intelligentsia and the State Department, a hunting down of communists and fellow-travelers with much noise and little success. The Federal Bureau of Investigation under Edgar Hoover was especially active pro-McCarthyism.

Lasswell himself was smeared in its records, and as a result the numerous scholars who used him as a reference had trouble obtaining security clearances for their jobs. A suspicious reference could play dominoes with a set of people. I had no trouble with my Top Secret clearance, but, besides referring to Lasswell, with whom I was close, I had several raunchy reactionaries rooting for my patriotism. Moreover, Lasswell's own great capabilities in psychological warfare and communications research were withheld from use. In the present context, it is worth mentioning that Lasswell and his acolytes did not close in on the Israel-Palestine-Jewish-US government quadrangle. He turned his attention to the reform of the hospital and medical policy system in his last years.

It worked also in reverse: a presumed reliable red-baiter was valuable to his friends needing a reference. A close friend and excellent scholar, George B. De Huszar, a Hungarian refugee (in some sense Jewish – he told the joke which in part went " ...one Hungarian a mathematician, two Hungarians a chess-game, three Hungarians: but that's impossible, he has to be Jewish!") – who died before his masterwork on Don Quixote was finished, incurred neurotic suspicions and jealousy against President Robert M. Hutchins of the University of Chicago regarding a girl he admired, extended his unreliable opinions to investigators and the *Chicago Tribune,* whose owner and staff hated the arrogant and beautiful man, and became a favorite point of reference for the McCarthyites in their search for communists and fellow-travelers.

The madness of the period of McCarthyism was as nothing compared with the plethora of lunatics that have become involved in the shenanigans of fellow-travelers, writers and uniformed spooks selling the Coming War Between Civilizations (Judeo-Christian vs. Islam), military cliques, media manipulators, eager warriors, every nation's and alliance's espionage and security managers, myriad expert commentators, and the politicians - American, to show how craven, and some of them Jewish, to show how meshugena, are the characters steering Spaceship Earth.

The key indicators of the garrison state are the warlike chauvinism of the media, the lopsided military spending practices of the government, the extent to which military advice is asked and followed, a preoccupation with national security extending into intrusions into private behavior, and the extent of warfare and dependance upon military solutions for political questions.

The US military has gotten stronger, but not necessarily more successful. It has some 800 bases around the world, but is still reaching out to construct new bases. In fact, one reason for its backing the independence of Kosovo from Serbia was clearly demonstrated by its undertaking in Kosovo the biggest of all US military bases in the world, Camp Bondsteel. The US population, however, has hardly grown more militaristic, mainly because it is so ignorant of the weapons and machines technology, and is always ready to demonstrate mildly against some new pretension of the military presence abroad.

It would seem that the US military is hardly needed, considering the absence of threat in the world. Certainly it would seem that NATO is useless unless it expands, as it is doing at present, to put up an aggressive posture in the Middle-East, extending even to China and Russia. A curious relationship exists with Europe. On the one hand, Europe is nothing but allies, on the other hand there is a competition and discordance of views respecting especially Western Asia. Europe lets itself be bullied with the help of the Italian Berlusconi party, the Polish government, French president Sarkozy, and in fact especially by the big boss, the USA.

❖ ❖ ❖ ❖

But let us begin with some remarks on the economics of the military, which have practically bankrupted the United States. Indeed if there were such a thing as bankruptcy for a government such as America it would be designated as a bankrupt. So committed is it to new expenses, that the government is no longer able to maintain properly its huge army, by replacing worn out equipment or preparing for warfare in outer space; many of its defense projects are quite theoretical and promise never to be put into practice. And as is well known, though the population is quite submissive, the country does not have the means, without hideously great borrowing, to invest in our failing social infrastructure, such as health, education and pollution control.

AIPAC, which watches these matters like a hawk, reports the latest aid program; "President Bush's fiscal year 2009 budget requests $2.55 billion in security assistance for Israel. The president's request marks the first year of a 10-year plan between the United States and Israel to gradually increase U.S. security assistance to the Jewish state to help it face increasing threats, including a potential nuclear Iran, daily Hamas rocket attacks, Syria's military build-up and the rearming of Hizballah. Under the agreement signed in August 2007, the $2.55 billion request will gradually increase until 2013, when it will level off at $3.1 billion per year until 2018. The President's request also includes $30 million to help Israel absorb refugees from the former Soviet Union and other countries."

The Department of Defense expenditures for the fiscal year 2008 are proceeding as larger than all other nations' military budgets combined. Just the current wars in Iraq and Afghanistan, which are not part of the official budget, spend more than the combined military budgets of Russia and China. It is expected that fiscal 2008 will exceed one trillion dollars in defense-related spending. In 2008, though figures never stay the same for long, the Department of Defense will be spending nearly

$500 billions for salaries, operations, and equipment aside from Iraq and Afghanistan. Then there are $142 billions in a supplementary budget for a global war on terrorism. There are another approximately $95 billions for hitherto uncounted war costs of 2007, and there is even an allowance of $50 billions to be charged to fiscal year 2009.

We are already approaching $800 billions for 2008 but there is a lot more. Other departments spend military funds without general knowledge, for example, $24 billions for the Department of Energy to develop and maintain nuclear warheads, $25 billions in the Department of State for extending foreign military assistance, a lot of which goes to Israel and its Arab and Muslim enemies. To a degree, the Israeli large military budget is financed by the United States as a way of concealing the fact that the US military hopes that any major engagements in the Middle East would be fought by Israeli soldiers and the US would not have to answer the deadly question: is the US army sending our boys to die for Israel? A question sure to provoke antisemitism.

Recruitment costs more money, because men are not stepping up promptly to enlist, and indeed, the quality of American soldiers agreeing to enlist has been dropping significantly. With Statehood would come a half-million apt recruits from among the Palestinian-Americans alone. And as a bonus, these would have been trained from the age of six to be soldiers in the ultra-modern fashion

– little Davids to sling a rock at Goliath, guerilla fighters, skirmishing gangs with all lines open to what they need when and where and how they need it.

The Department of Veterans Affairs gets over $75 billions, half of it for the care of the most seriously injured among the 30,000 soldiers so far wounded in Iraq and Afghanistan and near $50 billions goes to the Department of Homeland Security, an eavesdropper of lunar proportions. Then a couple of billions are spent by the FBI for paramilitary activities, some $38 billions by the Department of the Treasury for the military retirement funds, another $8 billions for military-related activities of the National Aeronautics and Space Administration and finally $200 billions in interest for debt financing of defense outlays. So the conservative estimates of persons such as Chalmers Johnson calculate well over one trillion dollars for fiscal year 2008. (This is enough to take care of the subsistence of the 3 billion poorer people of the world : 50% of all humans.)

The GDP (signifying Gross Domestic Product, not Gross Dissembling Product) of the European Union is slightly larger than that of the US, and China's is slightly smaller and Japan is the world's fourth richest nation. So one can see that the common view that the United States has unlimited resources to draw upon is false and when one thinks of how much the United States borrows abroad, that is, has a negative balance of payments, the figures become appalling. The current account deficit of 2006 was 811.5 billion dollars. The National debt has, with this unconscionable borrowing and spending, reached over $9 trillion by the end of 2007.

Congress dutifully raised the debt limit as it always does, so that more could be borrowed. The national debt has increased by almost 50% during the tenure of George W. Bush as President. The total value of the nation's plant and equipment and infrastructure is estimated by the Department of Commerce at only $7.29 trillions. This value increases too slowly because of so much spending on the military and so little expending on capital stock, modernization, replacement of the infrastructure, replacement of our capital assets. There is very little that can be done about all of these matters, certainly not by lowering the taxes on the rich. The American medical system, educational system and social welfare system are hardly up to the standards of the average developed country.

❖ ❖ ❖ ❖

David Ben-Gurion, in the years 1948-9, talked of ethnic purging with regard to the Palestinians and used sentences such as: "We decided to clean out Ramli," and so it was done.

Later he proposed to conquer Galilee and expel its 100,000 Arabs. By the end of the "ethnic war" of 1948-9, 6,000 Jews, 1% of their population, had died and a great many more Arabs.

When a group like the military tries to be unbiased, it will ask for over-performance from the possible victim of its bias. In the present case of Canaan, about 20% of the military would have biases against both elements, Israelis and Arabs, and are ready to move either way in a confrontation of prejudices. Normally, they would side with the weaker party that they can control, especially as they near the point where the other party, the Isreali in this case, is reaching near to the position of commanding power over the whole. For then it is that the threat is felt. Admiration turns to resentment, the weaker party is shored up and enlisted into a united party, the majority gets ready to act on any semblance of wrong-doing, double-loyalty, or error.

A Cossack division in the latter part of World War II reorganized to join with the Germans, abandoning their Russian affiliation, and were backed up against Switzerland in 1944 by the French First Army. We prepared a special leaflet to be fired over them, urging them to surrender, whereupon they would be treated well and in accord with the Geneva Protocols regarding prisoners of war. I wanted to tell them more: if I could only have said to them, " We promise not to turn you over to the Russians afterwards, but to let you live in France!" That would have brought most of them over without their weapons. I doubt that any of these collabos ever saw their homes and families again. Collaborators are treated roughly, too, in Israel and in Palestine.

Actually, the Palestinians have a strong propaganda line. But they can afford no psychological warfare unit to operate against the Israeli troops, illegal settlers, and civilians of the cities. With scarcely any means of warfare at all, a propaganda machine is unavailable. They could do much by posters and leaflets addressed to the enemy or dropped in their path.

Hatred of the enemy is also a strong handicap to the Palestinians. The threat of expulsion of the Jews and the destruction of Israel have an opposite effect to that intended, and is therefore inept. Insofar as the Israelis believe this, it incites a propaganda backlash, because then even the most pacific, conciliatory Israelis will put their shoulders to the wheels of the war-chariot.

Despite all the means they have to do well, the Israelis are acting increasingly worse, not better. They give evidence of transforming at any moment into fascism. If they feel the pressure rising much higher, they will explode the boiler. Most of this is real; some of it is a sham. But the pressure is in their minds and hearts, not on the ground.

Uri Avnery is the wisest of the critics of the government of Israel. On 15 March 2008, he is saying this about the media coverage of the events in Gaza: "These are, after all, the same media that danced for joy when the same government started an ill-considered and superfluous war in Lebanon. They are also the same media that kept silent, this week, when the government decided to hit the freedom of the press and to boycott the Aljazeera TV network, as punishment for showing babies killed during the Israeli army's recent incursion in Gaza... But for two or three courageous journalists with an independent mind, all our written and broadcast media march in lockstep, like a Prussian regiment on parade, when the word "security" is mentioned."

"(This phenomenon was exposed a week ago [my calendar] in *CounterPunch* by a journalist named Yonatan Mendel, a former employee of the popular Israeli web-site Walla. He pointed out that "all the media, from the *Channel 1* news program to the *Haaretz* news pages, as if by order, voluntarily use exactly the same slanted terminology: the Israeli army *confirms* and the Palestinians *claim,* Jews are *murdered* while Palestinians are *killed* or *find their death,* Jews are *abducted* while Arabs are *arrested,* the Israeli army always *responds* while the Palestinians always *attack,* the Jews are *soldiers* while Arabs are *terrorists* or just *murderers,* the Israeli army always hits *high-ranking terrorists* and never *low-ranking terrorists,* men and women *suffering from shock* are always Jews, never Arabs. And, as we said, *people with blood on their hands* are always Arabs, never-ever Jews." This, by the way, also goes for much of the foreign coverage of events here, says Uri Avnery.)

❖ ❖ ❖ ❖

Israel puts all Palestinians of the occupied territories, but not settlement Jews, under military justice, whose personnel are largely unqualified. Since 1990, its tribunals have processed over 150,000 Palestinians with scarcely a semblance of justice, aside of putting obvious serious offenders to death. The full extent of this execrable procedure of mass prosecutions was revealed in January 2008 in a report by a special voluntary group of Israeli experts, *Yesh Din,* which has supervised the work of voluntary Israel researchers from Israeli Non-Governmental Organizations (NGO's). In the years 2002 to 2006, military prosecutors filed 143,000 indictments on all sorts of charges. About 1% were for murder or attempted murder. No attention is paid to international law.

We are drawn to a comparison with Nazi behavior. The German Minister of Justice tried to control the processing of Jews and their possessions through the regular courts but the great number of cases was over-burdening the system, so we find him writing to Nazi boss Martin Bormann: "I intend to turn over criminal justice jurisdiction against Poles, Russians, Jews and Gypsies to the

Reichsfuhrer-SS. In doing so, I base myself on the principle that the administration of justice can make only a small contribution to the extermination of these peoples." (Hilberg, p 271) As in Israel later on, the pretense of due process of law could not be supported decently, so justice was turned over to the military where no trial at all was required, or as in Israel, the average trial became a matter of a couple of minutes.

The proceedings have received almost no publicity in Israel or abroad until now. The bundle of "rights" constituting the right of a fair trial were totally denied to arrested Palestinians. Trials are not public, not even for the family. Documentation is not available in Arabic, though all the accused are Arabs. Effective defense by attorneys is made impossible. All stages of a case are prolonged inexcusably. 95% of the cases end in plea bargains which really means confessions of guilt, despite the lack of all legal rights because the defendants cannot proceed without help in half the cases, and Arabic versions of proceedings were sloppily provided and untrained personnel did most of the translation. Palestinians between 16 and 18 are tried as adults, and are regarded as of their age at time of sentencing rather than when the offense was committed. Minors are not treated differently from adults. Torture is usual and practically ignored, as being impertinent to the trial.

Of 9,123 cases, concluded in 2006, only in 23 cases was the defendant found quite innocent.

Hearings before indictment rarely called any witness, and on the average prisoners were held for 10.2 days before the preliminary hearing. The average hearing itself lasted 3 minutes and 4 seconds. Hearing to authorize much longer detention while proceedings "progressed," took an average of one minute and 54 seconds.

Why do the Israelis bother to conduct these thousands of 3-minute illegal legal processes? They pretend they must do so for the record, they must deliberately fool themselves and fool the world. The great pride of Jews in America (my brother Edward was a founding professor of Cardozo Law School, a pro-Jew humanist) indeed everywhere, are their lawyers and judges, though too often trained in the hair-splitting rabbinical tradition. The process is one of psychological compulsion, even though all is so transparently unjust.

Prof. Nathan Leites, of the University of Chicago, in his lectures in the early days of the Shoah on political psychology, used to say this about the Nazis: they went to extraordinary lengths to explain themselves and record their absolute crimes. They were "Good Germans." They were Old Testament sticklers, too. They had to be correct! Everyone had to have his clean towel and soap before entering the deadly showers. The New England colonial ministers talked about being washed clean in the blood of the lamb. These Israelis of the Promised Land, too, I do not speak of all Jews – had to provide everyone with the semblance of judicial process, else they could not feel correct and proper.

❖ ❖ ❖ ❖

Israel keeps a large depot of atomic weaponry, guessed by experts to number in the hundreds, while refusing to provide any affirmations or denials, much less an inventory of them. In the 1967 war, already, Moshe Dayan as Commander-in-chief talked of letting fly an atomic bomb. He may also have been the trigger man in the USS Liberty massacre of those days. "We Jews have to behave like mad dogs," the glamorous warrior once said. There have been more of such ejaculations by Israeli leaders over the years. Few of us academic "schlemiehls" with our piteous, repetitious complaints can equal the rhetoric of such "meshugenas."

Part of the Israeli army, at this writing, is retaliating on behalf of Sderot, target of several Hamas missiles from Gaza. The town is one mile away from the Gaza strip, with a population of 20,000 of which over 3,000 left because of fear. The people are by origin recent Russian and earlier Moroccan immigrants, second class citizens, we note. They are among the half of the Israelis who reluctantly entered the country in the first place and would make happy Americans.

From 23 April to May 1948 typhoid germs were injected into the Acre aqueduct by Zionists to desolate the city's strong defenders. Jews were arrested in Gaza at the time for carrying malaria germs, this according to Ben Gurion's war diary of 27 May 1948. The men were executed. On 22 July 1948, Palestinian headquarters issued a report to the United Nations accusing Jews of using inhuman weapons in the form of bacteria and germs which were being grown in specially built laboratories. The labs are still there and working and barely denied. There is some mushmouthing about bio-poisons.

Avner Cohen in the Non-Proliferation Review of 2001 tells us that the story is true and the name of the operation of biological warfare was Shlach Lachmecha, quoting a letter of the military historian Uri Milstein.

We can be confident that the Israelis have biological weapons and would use them if thought to be expedient and that these biological weapons would presumably be turned over to US military safety control in the event of Statehood. (Depleted uranium weapons are also classifiable as biological weapons if the presence of deadly elements in air, water and living tissue is considered.)

Given the perilous large quantities of weaponry of all kind, including biological and atomic, the Congressional resolution granting Statehood to Canaan should require, aside from any approved State constitution, an inventory of all weaponry with the obligation of turning it over without compensation to the parallel US military authorities at the time the certificates of admission to Statehood are signed.

❖ ❖ ❖ ❖

The "sovereign sky" is 60,000 feet above a sovereign territory; this means little to the Israeli Air Force (there is no Palestinian air force nor airport; neither is allowed by Israel.) The war of the skies consists now of missiles that can leap over the rogue wall of Israel and of anti-aircraft guns. The sky battle is the one-sided 24-hour observation of all of Israel-Palestine by the sophisticated reconnaissance aircraft of Israel.

A new kind of warfare ensued: "Surgical killings" administered from above. During 2001 alone, the Israeli airforce conducted 5,130 sorties over the west Bank and Gaza, presumably Palestine territory. This included 600 flight hours in assault helicopters. 500 missiles were fired at Palestinian targets, about a third of the missiles achieving the 45 aerial target killings by which alleged Palestinian militants were liquidated.

Deliberately or carelessly, the Israeli armed forces have killed or disabled thousands of Palestinians, men, women and children, in most cases without hindrance, investigation, or trial, or for that matter without protest from the USA, except for a few voluntary humanitarian organizations. As one of a plethora of examples, a slaughter in the dawn of 8 November 2006, blew up the dwellings of two families, killing 19 persons and wounding 30, in Beit Beinun. The attack was effected by from 8 to 15 missiles and the Army Prosecutor decided that no investigation was needed. Archbishop Desmond Tutu was appointed by the UN to head a commission of inquiry, but was not even allowed to enter Israel.

The only effective kind of war is terror war. Or guerrilla warfare. Nuclear weapons and long range missiles cannot be used close-in. All tactics except guerrilla warfare result in unbearable escalation. All traumas of major weapons will be too huge to endure. Nor will the users and victims be able to go on to further tactics. They will be stuck in guerrilla mud. Therefore Palestine or the Taliban can endlessly fight off annihilation.

Still, here a disoncerting problem arises. Automatically, Canaan will become America's giant aircraft carrier. The planes the government would need would be to carry people back on leave, the only boats to carry freight. Mussolini and Petain will spin in their graves. *Mare Nostrum* will be the American Sea. The USA would control the Mediterranean as well as the Middle East, and this would be done without its sailors descending merrily upon Napoli and its soldiers upon Venice.

There was a time 1941 to 1944 when I, your author, worried every day about what is happening here and there in the Mediterranean. Too, Canaan would look into all directions militarily and the USA could withdraw all of its exasperating bases of NATO and aside beyond NATO. One of the significant results of getting rid of Saddam's regime was that the USA could get its bases out of Saudi Arabia, which had been necessary there in order to "keep Saddam in a box" and enforcing the sanctions strategy. Quietly, the US did indeed withdraw its bases from Saudi Arabia as soon as possible after overthrowing Saddam. Remember that the desecration of the Holy Land that hosts Mecca by the presence of American bases ranked, in Al-Qaeda's list of grievances, above our support for Israel. Therefore, leave everything to Canaan. Yahweh is in charge. No harm can come to Canaan.

That leaves China. We guarantee Taiwan to be harmless and unarmed and to give China a free port in Puget Sound, an area where so many Chinese are already usefully busy. We must make friends, real friends, for we have so much to do! I am writing in 2008; the situation has worsened for the Palestinians. Palestine has been allowed no sea rights or air rights by Israel. The people have often been starved for fish. Canaan will assume both the forces and the regular maritime and air operations, although practically all of these would be transferred readily into the type of Federal States system that now controls coast and air. The ports and seas would of course be open and friendly and hopefully productive.

❖ ❖ ❖ ❖

The Roman government believed it could enlist the German barbarians in its legions, and truly they did serve for a time dutifully. But in the end, they inculcated Roman practices into their own tribes and turned upon the empire to devastate it.

The USA politicians and military are arming and employing the Israeli military forces, thinking to avoid costs, harm, nuisance and public criticism respecting their own American forces. What, in the end, or has it already been occurring for many years, prevents Israel from realizing this state of affairs, using the US superpower for its own purposes? We cannot be sure of the Israeli, as some experienced US military connected with Israeli planning and operations will tell you.

Americans of German origin, who make up a quarter of the total population of the USA, are securely adjusted, vastly contributory to the nation's good, and law abiding. The Germans of Germany, while apparently pursuing the same progressive career as their US cousins, brought forth in the 1930s a dreadful Nazi movement that almost destroyed Europe, including especially the

European Jews. The Israeli must realize that there is nothing inbred in them that can keep them from committing collectively as a nation crimes against their neighbors and humanity as a whole. There is reason to believe that there exist in Israel meshugenas who are capable of committing massive crimes in the name of biblical prophecy or retaliation, eventuating in the preemptive or defensive firing of nuclear missiles.

The Israeli government was pleased when the USA attacked Iraq . For, not only was it destroying Israel's enemy, but it imitated Israel's war crimes.

Before the Iraq situation worsened, the daily Israeli newspaper *Maariv,* 25 March 2003, wrote: " ..over the years, the Americans and British have addressed reproaches at Israel for its way at fighting terrorism in the territories. Now, in Iraq, they are face to face with the civilian population and they have to take their turn in dirtying their hands."

Respecting the Russians, far from finding Israel a land of milk and honey, their immigration that in the 1990s built a number of towns, found itself in depressed circumstances, with little employment, living off army rations most of the time, with many single mothers among them, most of them poorly educated and losing a third of their purchasing power within two years of the accession of Benjamin Netanyahu to the post of minister of the economy in Sharon's Likud cabinet. Yet they voted heavily for Sharon and Likud, probably in hopes of being taken care of afterwards, a risky calculation. Army duty was irksome, but for many it was the better choice for a living.

It scarcely need be said, but Canaan's Palestinian-Americans would have the same rights as Canaan Israeli-Americans to enlist and serve in the American Armed Forces, actually the same rights they would come to possess to be educated, and pursue any career open to other citizens.

A Gush Shalom ad published in *Ha'aretz* tells us this: The Army's Chief of Staff said that the Israel defense force will "fight against terrorism until they sear the Palestinian consciousness." (That is, drive them crazy by burning, not the best way of reducing the number of terrorists.) Recently one of the chiefs of the security service said that the army's fight against terrorism "is like emptying the sea with a spoon." That same week (it was August 2004), the chief of army intelligence said that it is impossible to succeed by military means alone, since "Palestinian terrorism" is like "a bottomless barrel."

Uri Avnery writes in December of 2007 about the conference called at Annapolis by President Bush where he tried by all means to bring in a full representation of nations - says Avnery: "This week army intelligence announced that the chances of the Annapolis Conference are next to nil. Such a statement is proper for a political party, not for a military body. For 40 years now, the Israeli army fulfilled an eminently political function in the Palestinian territories. No wonder that it is now the strongest force in Israel."

The trouble is, however, that the Israeli army has not had a bright idea since it took over the Hagganah. They are great-grand-sons of General Ulysses S. Grant, whose applauded words, as his immense army attacked the outnumbered Confederates, were: "I intend to fight on this line if it takes me all summer!"

Massacres were common in 1947-8; the Israelis behaved no better than the German army as it ravished Poland and Russia in 1941. The scale of operations was much smaller but the methods were alike. The Israelis added an effective propaganda weapon, using loudspeaker vehicles to tell villagers in their path of the destruction already done, and what was to be done to them if they did not flee from their village.

A disagreeable feature of arms producers and armies around the world is their claim to be booming the economy, the GNP and GDP, whereas what they are really doing *à propos* human welfare, is manufacturing mountains of waste - to be spent, yes, on common goods, but in a well-run world, the "waste" would be the consumer goods and services, so there would be double the consumer goods and services (I do realize that certain military purchases, boots and potatoes, are usefully consumed and not doubling their cost, but I also recall, returning from the war, driving across the Southwest - Arizona? New Mexico? - and viewing parked B29 new bombers in the desert as far as the eye could see, a disgusting sight, and a few days later dozens of unused freighters tied up in San Francisco Bay.

❖ ❖ ❖ ❖

Israel has a large nuclear capability. Its presumed purposes are to deter a large conventional attack and all levels of unconventional chemical biological and nuclear attacks, to preempt enemy nuclear attacks, to support conventional preemption against enemy nuclear assets, to support conventional preemption against enemy chemical and biological assets, to fight a nuclear war and, the final, forfeit, or Samson option, probable suicidal destruction. The Israeli developed some low yield neutron bombs and "micro nukes."

This means, at the very least, that even should Iran acquire nuclear weapons, the equilibirum of terror would exist between Iran and Israel, as Israel's estimated 200 nuclear warheads(of which a considerable number are certainly right now aimed at Iran) would represent sufficient dissuasion against Iran.

Planners of Israeli strategy might well have considered focusing their nuclear and conventional fire on long range targets, for a strange but logical reason. Blasting nearby targets would endanger Israel impossibly. Better to threaten a far away ally of the nearby enemy so that the far away ally would press the near enemy to desist from nuclear or heavy missile engagement. Israel would, therefore, feel a little bit more comfortable nuking, or threatening to nuke, Iran than the close Iraq, let alone Syria. It is small consolation to permit any kind of nuclear exchange, unless one argues wistfully, no matter what happens, that it is likely that some small group of us will survive. I doubt that even Yahweh would want to clear out everybody on earth except his favorite tribe. On the other hand, there are people who would argue against me. Elohim composedly drowned everyone on Earth except a *shlemiel* family with an alcoholic father.

When all is said and done, Israel's nuclear weapons arsenal, like that of all other countries, is unspeakably dangerous. In the context here, we could say that the admission of Canaan to Statehood would consolidate the Israel and American nuclear arsenals, and by all odds the world would be safer, at minimum twice as safe. Whether speaking of Israel or the USA, religious fanaticism would be the most likely source of a nuclear war, a paramount reason for keeping the nuclear weapons out of the hands of rabbis, evangelical pastors, imams, and persons like President G.W. Bush, to whom God has spoken.

Consolidating the nuclear supply in the hands of one country, namely the USA, is perhaps as important as preventing Iran or another country from developing nuclear weaponry.

Not since the allied air forces destroyed recklessly the marvelous city of Dresden and similar targets of Germany when the war had actually been won, and not since the US air force strewed agent-orange, deadly to plants and animals, over settlements and plantations of the Viet Cong, has an army and air force so large, so well equipped, destroyed so much of a country as Israel has of Palestine, without public or even quiet protest by the USA, which went on continuously supplying deadly weapons designed for this very purpose, such as cluster-bombs.

The US and Israel military commanders and politicians are supposed to cooperate and do so. A survey of all instances of cooperation should however not only count and weigh them, but also conclude with an estimate of who initiated them and how aggressive they were in doing so.

Israelis, who need have little love for the United States, since they come from many other countries, have a not unearned reputation for producing more than their quota of reckless rogues. The US military has the contrary reputation of "keeping your nose clean" and "passing the buck".

Other factors being equal, the US military would tend to request questionable and risky adventures of the Israelis. And of course the

Israelis would tend to press for riskier alternatives for themselves.

This psychological difference, if true, is accentuated by the US military's control over the dispensation of funds needed in the postulated adventures. Ergo, the meshugena syndrome may be in part foisted upon the Jews, but not all of it.

Research funds for social psychologists to study the question are not likely to be forthcoming, despite the trillion dollars a year of military and war-connected spending of the next decade.

Kurdistan independence of Turkey, Iraq and Iran can be the provocation for a regional war, with the intensification at the same time of Israel's pariah status because Israel has been aiding Kurds (partly to hit at Iraq and Iran) which does not make sense (see for example Turkey) unless Israel wishes to get at Kurdish oil, possibly through a weak Iraq or possibly by double-dealing with the United States. Israel intelligence and military operatives have been working for some years in Kurdistan, training Kurdish commandos and running covert operations inside the Kurdish areas of Iran and Syria.

The United States is not too well informed about these matters. When Seymour M. Hirsch, writing in the *New Yorker Magazine* of June 28, 2004, inquired of an official of the CIA whether the Israelis asked for approval of their Kurdistan operations from Washington, the answer was a laugh, followed by: "Do you know anybody who can tell the Israelis what to do? They're always going to do what's in their best interest!" A top German national security official told Hirsch that: "An independent Kurdistan with sufficient oil would have enormous consequences for Syria, Iran and Turkey" and would lead to constant instability in the Middle East. It would be a new Israel - a pariah State in the middle of hostile nations.

❖ ❖ ❖ ❖

The pervasiveness of Israeli espionage in the United States invites separate names for its special parts. Sexpionage is one. Both in New Jersey and New York, State Governors lost their governorships over involvements with Israelis, one a homosexual lover, the other a procurer and head of a prostitution ring. Ernesto Cienfuegos in a web article on www.aztlan.net claims that ex-Soviet sexpionage agents of Jewish descent emigrated to Israel and worked for the Zionist government. The Soviets maintained a special school for them and such a training ground was set up at the Israel Institute of Technology in Haifa. Or so he says (or fantasizes).

The staple of espionage is placement in defense departments. There a sizeable Israeli record of espionage exists. Only the normal naive citizen can imagine that a country of all countries, so close, so dependent, would not bring in the largest group of spies, semi-spies, suspicious visitors, observers, and gatherers of confidential information. James McGreevey, a Catholic, Governor of New Jersey, found himself a lover, Golan Cipel. Cipel had held several jobs with Mossad and allied concerns and was an Israeli citizen. He was given a top job in the New Jersey establishment, overseeing security.

One beauteous woman, Chandra Levy, suspected of spying upon her lover, an American Congressman who was on the House Committee on Intelligence, went missing, until bones evidencing her murder came to light in Washington's Rock Creek Park, many months later.

Have I mentioned the incredible deliberate destruction of the unarmed American intelligence-gathering naval ship, the *SS Liberty*. Paranoid Israeli intelligence was probably provocative in unleashing Israeli weaponry against the Americans. I mentioned, too, the bungled attempt to fool Britain into reconsidering its decision to withdraw from the Suez Canal zone in the early 1950s, leaving the Egyptians in charge. American and British targets including Embassy buildings were bombed to pretend that Egypt was unreliable and hostile to the two countries.

Several of the highest placed Department of Defense officials had been under scrutiny and have been close to indictment for providing information and acting in the interest of Israel. In one case, the most powerful of Israel lobbies, AIPAC, found itself accused of plotting an operation transmitting Pentagon information about Iran to the Israeli secret service.

Actually, espionage prospers upon a broad base and systematic gathering of information. It need not be top-secret, or even illegal, and indeed can advertise itself as *pro bono publico*. The Jewish Institute for National Security Affairs (GINSA) can boast of a host of senior grade politicians, Washington insiders, and retired senior military officers, as its advisers, trustees and lecturers. It declares it is unique among think tanks in "putting the US-Israel strategic relationship first"; one unfriendly website writes, "GINSA makes no bones about the fact that it is recruiting an Israel fifth column inside the US military command. It would seem that most pro-Israel groups in the US and elsewhere strain to compete with each other in their successful conveyance of secrets to their home-country. GINSA sponsors junkets to Israel for retired officers, runs an exchange program for military cadets at West Point Annapolis and the Air Force Academy, with military institutes in Israel and affords lecture programs at many military institutions in the US where they bring in top Israel intelligence and military officials."

It seems that GINSA is eager to involve the USA in aggressive attacks upon practically every Arab state and propounds the idea of the Clash of Civilizations, subject of books by

Professor Samuel Huntington and authors of the Neo-Conservative network.

In the event of Statehood the Israeli army, air force, navy, and special services, such as Mossad and other secret service and military police, would need to be integrated into the armed forces of the USA. The Palestinian police would logically become part of the Canaan police; its other paramilitary could also be accommodated or pensioned off. The Hamas paramilitary and undercover bombers would have to disappear into the population. There would have to be a pardoning of all offenses committed during the war between Palestine and Israel. This has been done before, as in the Civil War; Confederate soldiers and officials were pardoned, usually after a short waiting period.

In WWII, without experience since 1918, the US Armed Forces needed to absorb and adapt to a dozen foreign military systems, British (themselves a motley assortment of Indians, Canadians, New Zealanders, Australians, etc.), French, Italian, Brazilian, and others.

When Italy switched sides from the Axis to the Allies, another ex-enemy establishment had to be accommodated immediately. I traveled throughout the area of the Italian surrendering and, without waiting for orders from the Allied Command at Caserta, I went to Sardinia, there making contact with an intact Italian parachute division that had ended the war waiting for an

Allied attack on Sardinia. I reported favorably upon its trustworthiness on grounds that it was monarchist and ready therefore to follow the king's orders – which were our orders. Its morale was good, even considering its late enmity. It was brought into line on the mainland, eventually.

Several reasons support a Palestinian loyalty also. In the first place, we are making the Palestinian people, for all the world to see, the biggest gift that could possibly be handed to them, absolute constitutional equality with all other Americans in what we consider the greatest nation in the world. Secondly, we give them "freedom of opportunity" to develop lives like those of most other Americans. If they wish, they can begin to "live their lives over again." Also, practically every abuse that they have suffered will cease and therefore almost every reason for reprisal or counter-aggression will disappear.

I would take nothing for granted, and point out that attitude samples and surveys of the Palestinian people plus a referendum will show the true feelings of the Palestinians and that these would demonstrate a very safe security setting for the juncture of peoples.

Finally, and backwards in time, the typical American company had its own melding pot. My original US Army company mustered Brooklyn Jews, Oklahoma Indians, Chicago toughs, Northern Great Plains Germans and Scandinavians, and a collection from a dozen other

Midwest backgrounds. So there is little to fear either in Jews and Arabs drilling and maybe going into battle together in the same units. White and Black soldiers had been segregated in the American army until after WWII when they were integrated. Only minor problems occurred. (I "requisitioned" three soldiers for my company for converting artillery shells. They turned up as blacks, hitherto segregated. They fitted like members of the family.)

If Israel were merged into Canaan State, its activities would not include any longer spying on the United States, for that would be spying on itself. Most of its espionage apparatus and personnel would be moved into the appropriate departments of the US national governments. One might even meet with the irony that a few of these men would have started life as espionage agents for the Soviet Union before working for Israel against us, and now working for us, and welcomed. Mossad would lose probably half its jobs and so too the other services. They should be treated well, else we would have a wild flywheel that would wreck the shop. Or maybe kill them? No, but with Mossad, as with all Canaan personnel transferred to American politicized jobs, an intensive psychiatric examination should precede the move, with periodic check-ups. An operation comparable to the Mayo Clinic should be provided. I have long advocated this screening for all aspiring and incumbent American politicians and public policy personnel. Considering that Israel operates relative to its size the most extensive espionage of any country, with America as a primary target, there would be a neat saving in eliminating its secret services.

Oil is a big Mideast issue and Statehood would bring the USA close to a monopoly on Mideast petroleum policy. The famous writer, Dr.Immanuel Velikovsky, a psychoanalyst, whose father had been an active Zionist, and who himself had lived and practiced in Israel before coming to America on the eve of our entrance into the War, was the author of brilliant works on ancient catastrophes and quantavolutions, and a neighbor in Princeton, New Jersey. I defended his most controversial books in my journal, *The American Behavioral Scientist*, in 1963 and afterwards..

During the War, besides his practice and his books, he had written articles in the *New York Post* defending the justice of the Jewish and then Israeli presence in Palestine, and wrote there also of the proximity of USSR to the Middle East oil fields. From the border of the USSR to the Iraq oil fields the distance is 215 miles, to the Persian Gulf about 550 miles. But, "In the atomic age, no war should be fought for any source of energy whatsoever." He urged the full development of atomic energy to replace oil.

What is also significant here is his theory of Collective Amnesia, a close predecessor to the presently important attention given to Post-

Traumatic Stress Disorder (PTSD). He asserted that the absolutely enormous catastrophes of early man, including, for example, the Deluge of Noah, had scarred mankind's brain and psyche forever, and left mankind liable to terrible aggressions when apparently provoked. Accordingly, then, he had to acknowledge that the Nazis were like everyone else, driven by unconscious causes. He considered the human race quite capable of committing suicide when aroused sufficiently by cultural hostilities. While supporting the cause of Israel, he was continuously fearful of the extremities of behavior that might explode in the situation. Yet, to explain the Nazis as victims of ancient suppressed memories required, in a conventional scientific world, that they be forgiven. Moreover, the rising temper of the Israeli-Palestinian conflict was pointing toward the idea that the Jews and Arabs were also unconsciously motivated by ancient catastrophes, such as errant comets striking the earth, to behave badly.

❖ ❖ ❖ ❖

So long as oil is important in peace and war, Israel is believed to be important as a force in readiness to contend with the Russians for the oil fields on behalf of the USA. Here is one reason why the US will back Israel in almost any folly. But, of course, if there were the American State of Canaan, the US would be in a much improved position *vis-à-vis* the oil of the Middle East, and, given its Palestinian component of Canaans, would be well set up to obtain the cooperation of the Arab states and Turkey or to influence compellingly their conduct.

Canaan State is ideally situated to pipe oil from the Middle East onto ships to Europe and America. It could compete successfully with Lebanon, Syria and Turkey in this regard. The fact that Canaan oil interests would be internal, not external, interests of the United States is a point of favor of Statehood.

Many Americans, Jewish and Gentile, draw comfort from accusing and condemning the large international corporations for the troubles of the Middle East. All such troubles - corruption, wars, shortages of oil, civil disturbances, coups d'état, terrorising of peoples, are the work of profiteers - so they believe. Declaiming this allows them to avoid thinking of any complicity of Israel and Zionists in generating any of the foregoing.

This line of argument allows Jews and Gentiles of radical or socialist persuasion to displace all blame upon dog-eat-dog capitalists, free enterprise, imperialists - adding to these the military as guards and enforcers. It is an old fashioned left-wing and communist conception of the world, and because there was no state of Israel, the Jews were kept out of this simplistic explanation - scorning the anti-Semites who claimed Jews had a big hand in all of this. This viewpoint and conception is of old-time Marxism, when Jews were in *shtetls* in Russia and pogroms were the order of the day.

Today it presents difficulty to political and social investigators who cannot discover the great corporate monsters on the front line against the poor countries. The large corporations do not own or dominate the Middle East oil states or any other oil states anywhere. They can bribe some of the politicians and bureaucrats with whom they deal and must do so, adding to the cost of production, to the price at the gas pump, and at the electric sockets. Logically a bribe is a common proper payment to an owner which must remain hidden. But the oil companies have little incentive to embroil the world in wars and revolution, because in the end they gain less than when conditions are stable, even if they do not actually lose the contest.

They find that their own government, here the USA, Britain, France *et al* are their greatest impediments, with armament races, spreading of political chaos, often in the name of democracy or "reducing corruption." Claims by left-wingers, ex-Trotzkyites, ex-Stalinists, or anti-globalists, seeking proof that ties various oil companies and construction companies to the U.S. government, forcing it to play an active role in grabbing oil concessions, are not completely persuasive in regard to the Near and Middle East.

These interests want peace and stability, at almost any price. As a result the glaring causes of warfare and possible gains become religious and tribal - chauvinistic causes that should have been expected to die out with the advent of modern times. The economic losses outweigh questionable military benefits. Human costs, furthermore, have become ever greater as human values increase; equipping and training modern soldiers is expensive; wounded or sick, their demands become heavy; dead, it is no longer a matter of dumping bodies overboard or spading dirt over them: they live on in shipping costs and pensions. Let me put it more strictly: over the century, no country in the world can gain more by military force in order to obtain oil, than it would stand to lose by all the human and material costs of warfare, even in the unusual case that victory followed by peace and order is assured. Any competent diplomacy or purchasing agent can, in a context of peace, obtain a country's oil supply (so long as the world market offers a supply). Is not Japan a case in point?

The military budget of the USA is planned in relation to the expected quantity and price of world oil production. Increases in price not only cause higher budgets for fuel and prices of all that the military buys, but also demands funds to conquer and to gain control over more of the supplies. If an economic recession of any kind should happen - and oh, is it going to happen! - the oil producing countries which invest their earnings in America and elsewhere will receive correspondingly smaller returns. (Note: December 2008. The recession has in these last weeks come crashing down upon America, and the whole wold straightaway.) All in all, ever more and more desperate disputes will break out as the purchases of industrially expanding nations like China and India bid for the oil. Science cannot yet tell us how much petroleum remains underground to be discovered.

Research can easily find oil-peddlers who hide behind the Shoah and vice versa. As Prof. Norman Finkelstein says, not only has the ghastly Shoah tragedy been publicized disgracefully to turn mourning into hoopla, but also reputations have been built in arguments over how many people actually died by executions and debilitation. The holocaust deniers must be dismissed, of course. But those other writers argue whether the total deaths number 4, 5, 7 millions or what? But other writers compare figures of how many, Roma, Russians, Poles, *et al* were murdered or died from imposed hardships off the field of battle. Some insist upon a distinction between soldiers and civilians, armed soldiers and prisoners of war, between deliberate killing and killing by neglect, etc.

The statistics are as usual poor or missing. I employ a five-million death figure for Jews. Some concentrate upon the Jewish figures believing them to be especially significant whether because of the high numbers or the special tradition in Christian countries of persecuting Jews which is thought different from mass murder, or out of simple nationalistic motive of hunnish barbarism of the horde, or mass killing and destruction of helpless cities like the allied planes over Dresden when victory was at hand, or the second atomic bomb dropped upon Nagasaki although the first atomic bomb upon Hiroshima was about to bring about the Japanese surrender.

❖ ❖ ❖ ❖

It is untrue that all war must be ruthless. There is little question that the ruthlessness of the Shoah was burned into the minds of the ultra-Zionists of 1947 and freed them from inhibition to do likewise in dealing with Arabs or anyone else including Americans or even Jews opposing them, as happened on occasion in struggles to control the war against Arabs and the ruling of Israel in the 1940s. (Such as with David Ben-Gurion, among others).

I ascribe much of the cruelty and callousness of the Israeli soldiery and politicians to this absorption, both conscious and subconscious, of hyper-machiavellism in all affairs of state including especially warfare. I have no experience with the workings of Israeli military enlistments and the minds of the soldiery. Yet I suspect that another reason for the cruel conduct of the soldiers as a matter of course may be owing to the large number of men and women, originating from the Russian and Polish life experience between 1930 and 1945, as transmitted by their parents and by their schooling - public, religious and cultural-social. Not only is this inherited barbarism, sadism, and destructivism carried by the soldiers and police who are in direct contact with Palestinians. It also marks the conduct of many civilians who are, openly or secretly, grimly pleased to witness the oppression of Arabs.

Israeli warfare is ironic. One war is being fought in the streets between overpowering Israeli weapons and Palestinian stones, small bombs and a few missiles. Meanwhile, across the way, Israel is playing in the big league of nuclear energy and high-tech warfare. Psychological warfare is going on all the time, with the Israelis and world Zionists again wielding enormous advantages.

Bruno Guigue was a deputy-prefect of Saintes, France, and an authority on Middle East matters. Upon the publication of an article on the generally reputable Islamic website *Oumma,* he was abruptly dismissed by the Minister of the Interior. The offense: lack of neutrality and failure to clear the article through channels. The article attacked Jewish lobbies for trying to block French participation at an upcoming UN conference on human rights and racism. The reasoning behind this attempt at blocking being that the conference would certainly condemn Israel for its violation of human rights and its refusal to obey international resolutions. (But is that not why such conferences are held?)

The Union of French Jews for Peace came to the defense of Guigue, saying *inter alia,* "Unfortunately this which the minister Alliot Marie (who fired Guigue) called violently 'anti-Israel' is the naked truth. The state of Israel has committed and commits war crimes on a daily basis."

The French Jews go on to say: "The way out of the Israel-Palestine conflict that one keeps presenting as very complicated rests in reality on a foundation that is quite simple: respect the Law, apply all the resolutions that the Israeli governments have violated with impunity for decades, assure the equality before the law among the peoples of the region.

"The principal obstacle to peace in Israel Palestine is the scandalous impunity accorded to Israel. The principal obstacle to civil peace in France is the inequality and the discrimination erected as a new morality. In seeking to gag all criticism, in attaching itself clearly to the side of the Israeli government, the French government is committing a very grave action. On the internal plane, it would like to criminalize all criticism on the part of its citizens and make an example by striking at the highest level: the prefects are commanded to keep silent and to fill their quota of expelling illegal immigrants lacking papers. [A controversial measure of President Sarkozy.] On the level of international policy, it engages itself in the unconditional support to the occupying power of Palestine. The French government turns its back to a 'just and lasting peace.'"

Should Israel succeed in expelling entirely the Palestinians, including the quarter-million living within its so-called legal boundaries as citizens, which would be logical and probable, it would then become a fully integrated world power. Thereupon its immediate obvious position would be as the Dominator of Arabia, meaning Lebanon, Jordan, Syria, Saudi Arabia, and Egypt... It would be the master of one of the several commanding corners of the world. But at the same time, if Israel expels the Palestinians en masse and against protests from all sides, it is likely to be hit by nearly complete ostracism and probably forced to commit deadly self-defeating attacks against Palestine, and probably have to engage at great cost other Arab neighbors, and force the United States to undertake most reluctantly its no necessrily forthcoming support. The Israeli people will live a veritably Spartan existence. And, too, atomic doom lurks. As the Israeli military expert, Professor Crefeld says, "our armed forces are the second or third strongest in the world. We have the capability to take the world down with us and I assure you that this will happen before Israel goes under."

If Statehood is arranged, it will, as part of the USA, become a friendly dominant power. But of course it will boast of a very different governing elite, a faction of a national and State U.S. political party, or perhaps only a mobile voting element as American Jews have been until now. From the viewpoint of the Arab nations, they will not be subject to the will of Israel, but dealing with a large mixed elite that they might well tolerate.

Again, let me state the contras: Israel has one of the world's strongest military forces. Not only does it possess vanguard weaponry - including several hundred nuclear war heads - with different modes of delivery, but has a well trained army to employ it. Even putting aside its atomic weapons, it would easily repel attack from any quarter. The only kind of warfare that will defeat it is ironically the combination of suicidal guerrillas, a few old-fashioned missile-launchers, and a hostile population. If Israel were to expel the Palestinian people from the region, which would take a full-scale, but brief assault, it would find itself in a peculiar state of being.

1. It would be hated worldwide and heavily boycotted.

2. It would lose population by as much as a third and would only survive as an obscene resort community.

3. There would be little eagerness on the part of the scientific, literary, artistic, intelligentsia to live in a disgraced country.

4. It would lose a large part of its Jewish constituency abroad, who would be disillusioned and skeptical.

5. A billion Muslims would be its sworn enemies (justified in any damage they would inflict upon it)

6. Many Americans would see in Israel's behavior not the romantic bucolic vision of early Zionism, but a machine shop where the mechanical god Yahweh unexplainably rules.

7. It would become a haven for crooked billionaires working at a variety of money manipulating tasks.

8. At some point in time, perhaps within 50 years, its government would be overthrown by a revolutionary movement that would seek every protection and benefit that world agencies would want to provide for it.

9. Considering how execrably the USA is presently proceeding in world and domestic affairs, a *coup d'état* in Israel might be associated with a *coup d'état* in America.

Then the American Garrison State would emerge beyond doubt.

POLICY SCIENCES AND TRAUMATIC DISORDERS

On November 27, 2007 President Bush launched a conference of some 50 countries and international organizations at Annapolis, Md., USA to approve the launching of an agreement between Israel and Palestine (Hamas excluded) which would promise to negotiate a firm peace accord in the near future. There was a great deal of conferring before and during the brief meeting by the leaders of the two countries and the USA, and the conference ended with a promise to go ahead with the two-state solution that had been long sought, usually called the "road map to peace."

A Declaration by the two governments ended the brief conference, with the many nations presumably standing by as witnesses and well-wishers. The Declaration contained the following lines: "In furtherance of the goal of two states, Israel and Palestine, living side by side in peace and security, we agree to immediately launch good-faith bilateral negotiations in order to conclude a peace treaty, resolving all outstanding issues, including all core issues without exception, as specified in previous agreements. "

Four months afterwards, a report issued by the organization called *Peace Now* claimed the death of the Declaration, listing a great many new constructions and settlements in the West Bank, all illegal. An explanation of this total fiasco suggests the following: The American government (that is, President G.W. Bush and his advisers) calculated that the whole world, if called into attendance, might now see how the US was always acting in good faith: they could witness that the principals were present, friendly, serious, ready to act, and to swear to bringing peace to the region.

Furthermore, the American leaders calculated that the two governments would take on themselves in good faith the full responsibility for peace, sworn in the presence of the world. (The United Nations, one would think, could do this job and was formed to do such jobs, so it was one more humiliation for the UN at the instance of the USA.) Too, the US, in the almost sure event of failure of the plan, would have shown "proof" that the two parties, Israel and Palestine, were to blame.

Spineless Abbas' Palestine shrugged its shoulders and played its part, the truly helpless split government, blithely solliciting the Moon, knowing that nothing would come of it.

As far as Israel was concerned, it went along for the ride. It is inconceivable that it took the charade seriously. This is proven by the almost immediate undertaking of a hundred or more violations, all with the most transparently false excuses, such as that some illegal construction had been started and that some repairs had already been underway before the conference. If the Israeli government actually meant what it swore to, then it must be among the most unreliable and incompetent governments in the world. This may be in a small part true, but also it was acting in bad faith, the two adding up to meshugena.

The most astonishing feature of the fol-de-rol was that the President and his advisers may have believed that the scheme could succeed.

Everyone of any consequence as a political scientist regards the Israel politicos and militarists – who govern the garrison state – as incorrigible. I think I have shown that all alternative policies to Statehood are incapable of clearing up the imbroglio. A self-respecting person, man or woman, must come around to asking himself "if this was done to my own people, would I join suicidal assault squads of the kind of Hamas and Hezbollah?" He might feel justified in doing so. Given that he could not manage that kind of action, what else could he do? What radical step apart from our advocacy of Statehood would he recommend?

Perhaps the answer is: we must ostracize the government - so long as it pursues its rogueries. Why forever fool ourselves? Why handicap ourselves? Many Jews of the world and their allied gentiles are supporting Israel to one or another degree, ranging from frightened   passivity to maniacal lobbying, pestering, funding, denying, propagandizing, demonstrating, pursuing violence, and performing any imaginable roguery against whosoever has seemed to be against Israel in any way whatsoever. This must not be.

❖ ❖ ❖ ❖

To pursue this "experimental thinking," it appears that only by becoming anti-Israel would a person become useful in this struggle to save our super-potent good name and a whole people of eight million from continuing to suffer a worsening from one year to the next of a suppression that has already passed sixty-three years. If the world did not crack down on the Israeli government when it imprisoned the total remaining population of Gaza Palestinians of 1.5 million persons, submitting them to near total deprivation, at the end of 2008, we know that the end of tolerance is near.

There is no recourse apart from Statehood - except strictly enforced anti-roguery laws, and I have little confidence in the systems that would be set up for such purposes. These would include, for instance, measures that impact heavily the Near East, laws limiting foreign and political activities of lobbies, bans on any U.S. private funding of foreign government military and political activities, close surveillance of persons carrying a Near East visa, psychological team examination at regular intervals of all persons in sensitive posts relating to the Near East, and quarterly reports of all tangible and intangible net and gross income of all individual U.S. Senators and Representatives and of their personal political staff. If it could be done, we would not want it to be done.

In all that has been written here, I have shown that for many reasons, Israel-Palestine must unite in order to avoid becoming a disaster area, cursed by the whole world for the troubles it has brought forth. And this Union should be the 51st State, USA, called Canaan.

However, the USA has lost in the eyes of the world its primary merits: more correctly, it has lost its reputation for being a fairly decent nation (for we know how often, from Indian and slavery days forward, it has played the role of the Rogue state).

Now how can we expect the Holy Land Israelis and Holy Land Palestinians to voluntarily entrust their lives, their fortunes and their sacred places to a disreputable America? Will it be enough that Jerusalem, the Holy Mount, Bethlehem, and other sacred sites become well-tended, respectfully guarded, open-to-all "Canaan State Parks"? I would say personally: "Yes, this is plenty."

I would say "Yes," again, judging from the motives, attitudes and behavior of all the Jewish and Palestinian characters of this book, inside Israel-Palestine and outside as Refugee Palestinians and Diaspora Jews (including the 3 million Americans who believe that they belong in Israel in heart and mind, if not - yet - in person).

I say "yes," the Israelis and Palestinians of Canaan will wish to become an American State for four reasons:

1)   90% do not bank their lives and fortunes and futures on the monopolistic demands of a religion. They want a secular State.

2)   Because the remaining 10% of claimants to sacred places, lacking support, will not resort to violence to possess the sacred places.

3)   Because the US can and will pledge itself to the UN to provide any necessary help to the State of Canaan to bring it along with the USA into agreement with the resolutions and requirements outstanding that apply to Israel and Palestine. This means the UN should, though it is not required to do so, conduct a General Assembly vote, in favor of, or against, the Canaan idea first.

4)   For all the reasons taken together in this book - reasons that are personally satisfying and reasons that bring

them into satisfying community among themselves and with the US and the world. Too, they can act in the knowledge – and nothing more satisfying could be imaginable – that they are, all of them, resolving the world's most desperate political problem and acting in that capacity, as the people who most responsibly and ably are initiating the creation of a new and better world.

The Israeli soldiers and officers and "commissars" are swelling and evolving out of their fathers and grandfathers – souls beyond judgement. And they are becoming these people of the past, feeling an urge to drive all these Palestinians to death and extinction, then turn on those who remember what is being done. The Israeli security forces have not peered into the mirror of the criminal beings that drove the millions to death - but they must try to see that if they do not change their way they must contemplate a similar mirror for the future reflecting themselves, not the Nazis and not a Moses either, who massacred but his thousands.

❖ ❖ ❖ ❖

The incredible human and material costs generated by what has now come to be widely regarded as an unnecessary, morally disgusting, aggression against Iraq began with the September 11 2001 destruction of the World Trade Center and part of the Pentagon Headquarters of the US Defense Department and the panic- stricken reaction of the American government, which has been since then proceeding with the specious notion that whatsoever mad course of action it pursued had by natural necessity to be good and democratic. To the contrary, at the same time its long history of misadventures shows what might have been avoided.

That Israel has accompanied step by step this reprehensible course cannot be denied. Not only the Israeli government and the Jewish public of Israel and the US, but the US government and unfortunately a particularly intense pro-Israel group in the Executive Establishment, cheered on by an Israel-supportive House and Senate. The evidence is clear, though the mass media suppress it and the press and pressure groups try to ruin whoever tries to publicize their representations of it.

❖ ❖ ❖ ❖

Canaan should be the first American State to dispense mental care to all its people, young and old. The percentage of the population begging for treatment is not greater in developed than in developing countries. For, whereas the stress and "poisons" of life in the poor countries are growing rapidly with the transformation of their economies and the radical changes in their family and cultural practices, the equivalents in the rich countries began earlier and have not peaked out.

Canaan's population has at least the prospects of health services volunteers from Israeli professionals and American collaborators. Lately in vast India a partly volunteer and partly professional corps is beginning rapidly to develop and spread its services from one village to another. With a billion people in line, the need there has hardly been realized until now.

The sickness lately named Post-Traumatic Stress Disorder worsens in proportion to the depth of the trauma. Terrorism is capable of educing a full register of degrees of acuteness of trauma. It can cause grave PTSD. When we ask what symptoms are prevalent in PTSD, the answer is across a broad range. The theory of *homo sapiens schizotypus* that I have put forward elsewhere brings out paranoia, social aversion, fear, anhedonia, obsession, orgies of pleasure and aggression as effects of traumas that have severely stressed the personality. Both natural disaster and human strife can originate and accelerate PTSD and its consequences.

Israel and Palestine have both suffered massive traumas within the past half century. Israeli have carried a heavy trauma from the Shoah, that would tend to render them as sufferers beyond experience in regard to the Palestinians. But, on the other hand, the Palestinians have been submitted to so many severe deprivations inflicted upon them by the Israelis that one might expect and consider the level of PTSD in the two cases to be comparable. And let us not forget that the trauma of the Shoah is one, two or tree generations removed from almost all Israelis living today, whereas the trauma of the Palestinians is present and on-going, and involved three if not four generations of Palestinian people living today. Whereas the direct Jewish trauma lessened in 1945, that of the Palestinians rose sharply beginning in 1947. In fact, in the few studies that have been presented, there does appear to be an excessive PTSD level in both populations when compared with outside normal populations less traumatized recently by natural and humanly provoked disasters.

The already high PTSD rate in both Palestinian and Israeli populations is ever-increasing. Fright, hatred, injuries to self and intimates, gory scenes, abusive treatment, eternal foreboding, anxiety over minimum food and drinking water, anticipating new blockades and penalties, panic, fighting within one's own groups aside from the enemy as a whole: probably the only item of stress missing here when moving from Palestinians to Israelis is the availability of food and water and a lesser expectation of deadly explosions.

The leaders of the depression-anxiety therapy movement in Goa (India) have found that the symptoms and cure are the same East and West, and in Black Africa. Apparently more and more of the seven billion humans on Earth find coping with modern life impossible alone. Far from reducing their peoples' life problems, the leaders and upper classes, themselves growing less sane with the times, are conducting their immense flocks into a desert with climate warming to precede them.

Emile Durkheim, an eminent French sociologist of the late 1800's-early 1900's, discovered surprisingly that the poorest and the richest of society committed more suicides when times were bad. He determined that both groups suffered from "anomie," a general mental instability. To them and to the people as a whole, material welfare was less important than psychic welfare. As their society became distrubed they felt less protected and more deprived of social affection, that is "neighborly love." They were, he wrote, suffering from "anomie," a mental imbalance whose symptomology resembles that of PTSD. In the 1950's, the research of Sebastian de Grazia applied the concept f "anomie" to governments, demonstrating that whole peoples are cast into depression and disorderly behavior when the political order becomes disturbed, untrustworthy, and turbulent.

Reassurance, love and security are effective therapies for reducing high levels of PTSD. Insofar as Statehood implies and actually brings on large "doses" of these conditions, we would recommend it then as carrying results that are significantly beneficial in these regards. Statehood, thus, becomes a form of psychotherapy.

The history of the Iraq war, now probably midways after five years, and that of Afghanistan, too, and the looming likely violent conflict involving Iran as well, have revealed an America that is as close to economic disaster and diplomatic ruination as it has ever been. Within another five years, even if the US does not attack Iran, every indicator of order and welfare in the world's list of major troubles will be worsened.

Washington's governing, lobby, and media gangsters cannot escape incrimination for this world-wide-wounding.

❖ ❖ ❖ ❖

At this writing, no one can predict how much longer the Iraq War will last. Some measure of its cost thus far has been made available. According to William Polk (pp. 203-4 of his *Violent*

Politics) "as of June 20, 2007, at least 3,521 American servicemen have lost their lives, and about twenty-five thousand have been wounded of whom half will never fully recover and many will spend the rest of their lives in hospitals. The human costs to Iraqi are nearly incalculable: perhaps as many as 601,027 (according to a study made by the Johns Hopkins School of Public Health) were killed between March 2003 and July 2006.

"The Department of Veterans Affairs has determined that up to October 2006 about one in five soldiers who served in Iraq has been 'at least partly disabled,' more than one hundred thousand have been granted disability compensation. About two hundred thousand were expected to claim compensation. About two hundred thousand of the troops who have served in Iraq have suffered severe psychological damage or post-traumatic stress disorder (PTSD); in June 2007, a Pentagon mental health task force reported that 38 percent of soldiers, 31 percent of marines, and nearly half of the National Guard and reservists needed mental health treatment. Even that number may be low because the numbers requesting help have so overwhelmed existing facilities that large numbers are being denied treatment.

"Another fifty thousand or so have suffered concussions that will afflict them with memory loss, headaches, and confused thinking probably for the rest of their lives.

"Neurologists predict that hundreds of thousands more – at least one in each three soldiers who have engaged in combat for four months or longer – are in danger of blindness, deafness, or mental impairment. As one reporter put it, blast waves causing traumatic brain injuries 'can leave a nineteen-year-old private who could easily run a six-minute mile unable to stand or even to think...' Crassly put, they will not only be unable to contribute fully to American society, but will be a burden on it...

" Another number of Americans... will possibly develop cancer or will conceive children who will be born with severe defects because of exposure to the depleted uranium used in artillery shells and bombs."

According to the Italian Military Registry of Health, over 3% of the 3,000 Italian soldiers serving their short term in Iraq died from DU cancer within a year of exposure.

Actually, the record already is appalling with regard to returned soldiers and their children. We have poisoned our own men: bio-amicide.

Almost two million Iraqis - about one in each thirteen - have fled the country. These were of the Sunni people who are 1 in 3 or 4 of the population. Over 1.5 million Iraqis have become internal refugees.

Massive overcrowding, widespread physical destruction of the country, deadly pollution (also from depleted uranium weapons) are everywhere.

❖ ❖ ❖ ❖

Political science is the systematic science of power and governmental activities. Politics is the practice and applications of political science. Policy science is making decisions and plans of politics. Making up a new State calls for all the latest ideas and skills of all branches of political science. The lessons of history, the future as we see it, demands a new strictly objective history such as has been written for the past century of Palestine and Israel. This history demands new methods of collecting and analyzing data, new machinery for handling the data, and critical judgements justified by the data.

One of the most useful guides to fashioning properly a new State of Canaan is the simulation of its structure and operations. For example we wish to know how many houses and living space are required for a population that has not yet arrived and will be increasing and decreasing predictably over the locations where it will settle, be it rural Israel, the towns and cities of Israel and Palestine, the several likely locales of the continental USA: We make the most correct possible estimates of how many of who occupy what space where and at what cost, requiring what living supplies, transportation, leisure time space, educational and health facilities and all other psychic necessities, structural and functional. What institutions are proposed and to be constructed.

❖ ❖ ❖ ❖

Public temper management on a grand scale is called for. From the start of agitation for Statehood, waves and episodes of paranoia must be systematically observed and treated. Teams of collaborating psychoanalysts and ethical scientists are to be formed to treat paranoia, but also sheer hostilities. Terror incidents need to be predicted and prepared for. Panic is to be expected from time to time as the processes of assimilation and adjustment go forward. The Public Temper has to be continuously gauged and controlled. Boycotts are to be employed from time to time versus hostile groups and activities.

Information has to be supplied abundantly to the public, reaching into all niches. This is, of course, propaganda, that is, information stressing the need for attitudes favorable to Statehood and integration of Canaan into the Union. Included is a vitally needed moderate history of Israel-Palestine over the past century and proof of the legitimacy of the presence and sharing of the land by Jews and Palestinians.

The PTM team has also the task of exposing political chicanery, media manipulation of contra-state propaganda (exposing profits made by the elements in the potential State that oppose its emergence). Too, a heavy blocking of all efforts at justifying the weapons industry and its ethical degradation of a nation. National character is a tricky topic that nevertheless attracts universal interest. A century-old joke of the Imperial age tells this: "An international contest for the best book on the elephant was held. The entries arrived. From England came a book: *I Hunted the Elephant.* From Germany another titled: *An Introduction to the Metaphysics of the Elephant* (Three Volumes). From America, too, arrived a book: it was called: *Bigger and Better Elephants.*

The study, training in, and application of national characterology are part of the job of PTM: one would imagine that the study of anti-Semitism must be complete, so many thousands of articles have been written on the subject, but it has not gotten into practice beyond a few rules for the regulation of public expression.

From 1920 onwards, ladies and gentlemen were trained to avoid generalities about nationalities, and especially to avoid derogatory remarks about a people. It has come to pass, to take the relevant case, that the word "Jew" cannot be spoken without ears pricking up: antisemitism is expected and suspected. "Give me any sentence a person utters containing the vocable "Jew" and I'll expose to you an anti-Semite." It is not laughable that a half-billion Arab Semites of the world are practically by definition "antisemitic."

Nor is it jolly that millions of American fundamentalist Christians who were disgracefully raised to be anti-Semitic and anti-Jewish for reasons of responsibility in the crucifixion of Jesus and more ancient hostile allegations are, for now, insanely strong supporters of Israel. They believe that, in the ultimate struggle that will soon bring an end to the world, Armageddon, Jews must return to Israel there to be joined by all Christians and converted to Jesus-Christ. Whereupon all will be judged by the Almighty God and good Christians will go to Heaven.

Practically all sociologists will agree that people who believe themselves to be Jews may be defined as Jews. And allowances are to be made for a few of these who disclaim or renounce their Jewishness. It is typical of some persons in every sizeable group to assert "I am a free person," "I don't belong here." Or "I wouldn't join any country club that would have me," in the immortal words of Groucho Marx, scion of Alsace, source of many great men (including Captain Dreyfus, Albert Schweitzer and the map-maker who named America after Amerigo Vespucci.)

It is scientifically permissible and useful to combine cultural background with a life-style and speak of an "American Texas ranger," or "American go-getter," or "American suburban housewife" and mean something rather more special than "a Nigerian ranger," or a "Hong-Kong go-getter," or a "French suburban housewife."

So I never think of Jews as a hard-and-fast character but sometimes one or another of types like these: "an orthodox Jew," a "Reform Jewish Chicago doctor," a "Brooklyn communist Jew," a "Jewish" Princeton professor of mathematics, an Israeli politician, a Jewish broker, a Jewish salesman. A Jewish civil servant, a Jewish refugee from Nazism, a Jewish mother, a Jewish entertainer, a Jewish political manager, a Jewish media producer, etc. All, no matter how assimilated to an average (30% to 70% typical, let us say) has to relate to "Jews" in some ways more or less important (names, ethnic origins, occupations, circumcision, Sabbath observance, etc. including a simple awareness, a self consciousness that is Jewish). Then one thinks of a number of statistical features: wealth, income, proneness to take initiatives, IQ scores, liberality of social and political viewpoint, membership in voluntary groups, etc.

Most political scientists fled from the firing line as soon as the first shots were fired. Not they alone. Social scientists, indeed scientists generally, showed their backsides. Old-fashioned stubborn civil-rights advocates and humanitarians have provided the main defense of the persecuted Palestinians. They, and rare spirits - Uri Avnery, Mazin C. Qumsiyeh, and Norman Finkelstein as examples - hold fraudulent history at bay. There is an organized "peacenik" movement in Israel, like *Gush Shalom*. They get financial and moral support from abroad, so as to be able to hold demonstrations and pay for publicity. Thanks to them, most Israeli roguery is publicly noted. They find Palestinian counterparts who are fewer, yet quite needed to round out teams for addressing the many conflicts, potential and actual.

Nobody (at least not I) find people any nicer than some 40 Mormons whom I have met in my life. Their founder, Joseph Smith, told a "tall story" and the Church of Latter Day Saints resulted, which occupied and built up Utah and parts of adjoining States. The life of Joseph Smith reminds one of the life of Mohammed, the Founder of Islam. If I can love and understand Mormons, why not Muslims (which I do) and Jews (which I most surely do). An attractive Mormon, governor of Massachusetts (far from Utah) ran for President in the primaries recently. Massachusetts is a State fat with Catholics. How can anyone convince me to scorn Palestinians? Why? Because they don't shave every day of the year? (Especially as Israel sees to it that in many places, water is running only a few hours a day.) We know Jesus washed and grew a beard, also that he was a pacifist and didn't like moneylenders much. Am I to scorn him because he hated warfare, grew a beard larger than mine, and would rather have given money to me than lent it?

❖ ❖ ❖ ❖

The idea that Israelis and Palestinians cannot make a state together is ridiculous. Given the will, intelligence (scientific skills) and a little time, and their average compatibility in Canaan would exceed the average of various other States. Several field studies support this opinion.

Canaan will supply a large number of US citizens who have had excruciating personal and/or group experiences, to which no counterpart exists in the USA. From the start Canaan, USA, Sponsors movement (CUSAS) should erect monuments, fly the C flag and prepare secular songs. Their endless painful experiences, their awesome knowledge of the depths of sorrow and atonement, will influence the whole of America to reject the politics of racism and violence.

The Lord "spake unto Moses face to face, as a man speaketh to his friend." (Exodus 33:11) This was after, not before, Moses had done his friend the favor of exterminating, with his Levite helpers, 3000 of his tribesmen, including "brothers, friends and neighbors." Moses was a killer on a large scale. He ordered the extermination of the Moabite people who were greeting his Hebrew flock too warmly, lasciviously, that is! But the genocide was finally forestalled by his own men who instead put him to death. So wrote Ernst

Sellin, to whom Sigmund Freud was indebted in *Moses and Monotheism,* and so this author as well, who pictured the scene in *Moses and the Management of Exodus.* How the "healthy" old man, enraged at the commingling of Hebrews and Moabites at Beth-Peor, sent the Levites to massacre the revelers of both tribes, to the number of many thousands. ("David slew his thousands," and so did Moses, and so did the British machine gunners of WWI whose monument with these words stands proudly in Hyde Park, London.)

I note this approved conduct of Moses and the Levites (as did Machiavelli, too, in his *Discourses*) and wonder whether the many millions to whom the Old Testament is literally true, have not within their subconscious justification for the same behavior - that of Hitler, Stalin and Mao. I recall that the Israeli hero, Yitzak Rabin, held forth in his spare time at a little social seminar devoted to Moses and killed his complement of people when called upon, or decided that the occasion was right. The trauma of Beth-Peor was tremendous, says the Bible, and the many traumas of any people who have held on consciously, religiously to traditions so long, maybe over 3000 years, cannot but mark them as indelibly suffering from Post-Traumatic Stress Disorder. And, respecting Yahweh, as the vulgar saying goes: "With friends like this, who needs enemies?" Moses has little in common with the humanist, modern Jew.

Hard-core Zionists have been ruling Israel for 60 years and more. Of these Zionists in Israel there are probably a half-million, in America a million. They could be rated on a scale. A hard-core Zionist is any Jew (or Gentile) who scores 3 or more on this scale:

1. If Israeli or even if not, and if Zionists are in charge, serves Israel-First before country and humanity.
2. Harassed others willingly and engaged aggressively in some Israeli roguery.
3. Has contributed non-charitable money in large amounts to Israel.
4. Has discriminated invidiously vs. Palestinians and humiliated them as a matter of course.
5. Has been active in Pro-Israel pressure groups and propaganda.
6. Is secular and morally self-serving.

An academic who has spent a long time reading and moving about, meeting many Jews, will have learned to distinguish many types. Jews have been everywhere and done everything. I was surprised to discover upon landing on the Island of Naxos in 1968 a somber little synagogue of the onetime Jews of Naxos. When the Turks went to war with the Russians in 1877-8, a Russian warship entered Naxos harbor and looted the island, taking, among other valuables, all of the Jews, who were carried off and never heard of again.

❖❖❖❖

A policy maker or a writer needs to bear in mind the many roles and connections of Jews. They are unquestionably the most varied nation in the world (of course, the same perspective of multiplicity should accompany thought about every human grouping). All of the following groupings, and more, have differences that one ideally ought take into account when factoring Jewishness into a situation:

1. Rabbis
2. Ritualistic Orthodox cults
3. Orthodox
4. Reform
5.Various small sects (Jews for Jesus-Christ, Reconstructionists, e.g.)
6. Non-practicing Jews (god-believing)
7. Atheistic Jews
8. Half-Jews by mother - practicing
9. Half-Jews by mother - non-practicing
10. Half-Jews by father - practicing
11. Half-Jews by mother - non-practicing
12. Related by marriage to Jews - female
13. Related by marriage to Jews - male

14. Cousins of any of the above
15. Children of 8 to 11 of the above
16. Employers of Jews
17. Jewish employees of gentiles
18. Employees of Jews
19. Jewish employees of gentiles
20. Russian and Polish Jews
21. Hungarian Jews
22. German-Austrian Jews
23. Other European Jews - French, Alsatian, etc
24. Arabically cultured Jews
25. Muslim-cultured Jews
26. Various Asian Jews
27. Imperialistic-chauvinistic Jews
28. Ladinos of Salonica
29. Pre-WWII Jews of Palestine
30. WWII crisis Israelis
31. Post-WWII Israelis
32. Palestinian Israelis
33. Yemenese Jews
34. Ethiopian Jews
35. Law and government Jews
36. Medical and Health services Jews
37. Academic and research Jews
38. Military Israelis Jews
39. Financially occupied Israelis and international Jews.
40. Communist Jews
41: Media Jews
42. Entertainment and magician Jews
43. Determined leisure amateur, rich or poor

44. Artistic Jews
45. Literary Jews
46. Musicians and composers
47.Mamzers
48. Jewish Refusniks (denial of Jewishness)
Et al.

No Jew belongs to only one category, but to two or more. Our purpose in creating such a somwhat silly list is to remind ourselves how variegated Jews are, with probably half not expressly qualified to be called a Jew or call herself or himself one. Yet there are some definable psychological and behavioral traits that are designated by each number and hardly in any other.

Because of social exclusion, a caste system, ghettos, self-defense, dislike of practices and traits of gentiles, tragic historical events (e.g. riots, pogroms), commercial and financial in-group preferences (i.e. advantages in making profits), freedom from crucial restraints (e.g. in money-lending at high-inerest rates and pawn-brokerage), genealogical intimacy and endogamy, shared experiences (the shtetl, the Shoah), special religious practices (e.g. the Torah, dietary rules, circumcision), cosmopolitanism (and reclusiveness), even a small Jewish population will have within itself an expansible and contractible version of a large society within whoe boundaries it functions. With all of this, a truly integral Jew is like Robinson Crusoe, a "stand-alone," self-sufficient, and, too, like an embryonic stem cell, which can grow into any anatomical organ.

Meanwhile, Palestinians, if regarded as an isolated group, and actually as it has been for 60 years, from the larger Arabic world, would not possess so many different developmental potentials as would be found in a group of isolated Jews. They would assimilate (that is, become "100% American") more quickly and irreversibly, for whatever that may be worth. Palestinian-Americans might be happier, but probably not as "successful" overall as Israeli-Americans.

It must be clearly understood that the element running Israel and its American-Jewish power-centers is quite small in relation to the whole number of Jews and Jews-related people. I would guess about three in a hundred, excluding children.

❖ ❖ ❖ ❖

The loss of loved ones and destruction of social networks has been observed to be far more damaging in causing PTSD than loss of limbs or otherwise physical disablement.

Of the thousands of psychiatrists in the US, a good proportion is Jewish and of all the psychiatric, especially psychoanalyzed, patients relatively many are also Jewish. Rare are those specialists who have reported fixations or even attention to the effects of Israeli events on the

Israeli or Jewish conscious or unconscious. Considering the extremely high levels of interest in their progress, this asks for explanation.

I would expect several findings:

1. That very many Jews and quasi Jews are driven into neurosis.

2. That usually psychological defenses are so strong that the events are easily and quietly mythicized and justified in secular terms, and wherever possible in historical terms reaching back to the Holy Land and Promised Land biblical archetypes, and the Shoah.

3. Favored therapies are rationalizations as here above and in Machiavellian terms: "power politics," "self-defense," subconscious displacement of aggression from Nazis to Palestinians and gentile antisemitism, including the special category for Jewish antisemitism, the "self-hating Jew."

These ideas require elaboration and proof, which is beyond my possibilities here, if only for the aforesaid conjunction of patients and doctors in the same psychic binding. Psychological defensiveness is a heavy promoter of aggression. Any observer following the Web on the keywords of Jews, Israel-Palestine-Shoah-wars-Zionism and related terms will discover an astonishing abundance of material. Even allowing for the Jewish affiliation to the *Word* (the *Torah,* etc.), there is gross 'excess.' The battering received by persons, both modest and famous, for indicating unsatisfactory Israeli conduct is terrific. The People of the Law and Charity disappear as in a puppet show, and the Biblical Devastator of the Philistines pops up. We recommend that the Psychiatric Associations plunge into the fray – with small hope that they will do any more than the Political Science Associations, nothing.

Special steps need to be taken to reinforce the spirit of collaboration and mutual respect in Canaan (not that America as a whole does not need much education in compassion). A certain proportion of people have always been taught to dislike or suspect certain persons and groups. In Canaan, certainly over 75% of the people, Jews and Arabs, have been taught contempt and hatred. So Canaan State will need potent and universal help in the learning of compassion.

Recent studies have shown this to be possible. "Specifically, concentrating on the loving kindness one feels toward one's family (and expanding that to include strangers) physically affects brain regions that play a role in empathy," writes David Biello in *The Scientific American* (March 26, 2008). "There is such a thing as expertise when it comes to complex emotions or emotional skills, such as the one of cultivating benevolence," says Antoine Lutz, a neuroscientist at the University of Wisconsin-Madison who led the study. "That raises the possibility that you can train someone to cultivate this positive emotion."

Many Jews want to hold on to their "history:" they have more of this tenacity than most other Americans. However, a number of other American groups feel the same way. But usually they hold on to a history of culture - Greek, Italian, German, Irish, Spanish, etc. A culture is not so obsessive-compulsive. God-obsession helps their hold on their "history."

The birth of Zionism came at the climax of nationalistic ideology. The core-Zionists became and are crazily patriotic for an invented state. They fed Arab nationalism, then fought it, and so on, back and forth, each intensifying the madness of the other.

University of Toronto researchers, an Israeli, a Palestinian and their Canadian PhD supervisor studying suicide bombers, found them to be "normal," meaning "understandable," motivated by desires for personal revenge, for territory, and not heavily for religion. The supporting team weeded out psychotics.

Politicians, political psychologist Professor Harold D. Lasswell noted in the 1930's, are wary of psychiatrists, because they have much to conceal. His presidential address to the American Political Science Association pointed up the problem of neurotic politicians and appealed for some kind of psychological clearance for them – a kind of license examination before being allowed to garner votes as a candidate for election. A constitutional provision of the Canaan Constitution would break new ground by calling for a mental, ability, and psychological test that would be required as a qualification for candidacy to public office. Many occupations demand such tests. The problem is not without delicate features. Properly propagandized and administered, the certificate of character or psychic eligibility for elective office would become a universally sought-for badge of honor, even among a great many persons who would not necessarily run for office.

❖ ❖ ❖ ❖

There was little heroism in the Shoah. And there was little room to express heroism. Considering at least five million Jews killed by the Nazis, the same number of Russian soldiers were killed by the Nazis and Germans and three times as many wounded plus 6 million starved, murdered, and 20 million driven from their (destroyed) homes. The Jews were almost all passive victims, who went from arrest, round-up, transport to camp (like many other millions of displaced persons from England to Siberia, Norway to Crete).

I can think of one reason, and sometimes I think it may be the justification for the state of Israel. Israel is a living giant aggregation of permanent mourners for the Jews of the Judeocide. The Russians who died have a nation to mourn them and memorialize them. Alas, this is not enough, and too much. Mourning is not enough of a function to justify a state. Indeed, it can make a rational modern benevolent state impossible. Something like this process has happened with Israel. No nation in the world but has its mourning function.

And the Jews and Israel cannot, should not, expect the world of nations to accord to it too much more than its special quota of memorialism, for they are busy with their own unjustly as well as normal deceased legions. (This, you will recall, was the main point made by Arun Gandhi.) At this writing, Israel is celebrating its 60th Anniversary as a declared nation-state. Its main claim to glory is still that its people belong to the Great Club of Survivors (even though most Israelis have not been survivors of the Shoah, or even descendants of it, but just normal survivors, as we all are, in a sense).

Perhaps there is a certain truth here, that the state of Israel was founded, not for the specified reasons advanced by Zionists, but to provide a gigantic prayer rug for mourners.

And perhaps none of the other reasons to justify its significance convey any greater meaning. Certainly, making life a misery for eight million

Palestinians over many years does not justify Israel or give it reason to celebrate its first 60 years. Let me put my theme in yet another way: Only the U.S. State of Canaan, as we propose it, can restore the Jews and give them the glory that they wish and, yes, deserve.

Let me speak now of assimilation. Canaans will become Americans overnight. Note how Congressmen, newspapers, and pastors contemned while few praised earlier immigrants. Employers fought vigorously, however, to bring in the poor uneducated new immigrants: they made the best workers.

Then they, because the political system permitted it, somehow - it is a real mystery - these new strange people pulled themselves together, sent for their wives and mothers, found living shack or two rooms and a fire-escape and within 20 years were for all ordinary purposes assimilated.

We can be sure that this same miracle of social congregationalism will happen to our Arabs from the 51st state. A third of them will accomplish this miracle in the USA, two-thirds at home in the state of Canaan or another place. Whether they will be isolated, in some remote area of Canaan as has happened in the States with British, Blacks, Germans, Mexicans, *et al.,* they will take several generations for full (i.e. typical) assimilation.

Ignorance of events was pandemic during the Shoah years. When I read the thick precious volumes of Prof. Viktor Klemperer's diaries of

Dresden, covering the years of Hitler's rise to power and of the war, I could see that the perception which he and the Jews among whom he was numbered paralleled uncannily my own state of knowledge from 1933 to the destruction of Dresden and the end of the war in Europe in 1945.

Some of us, as I, at the University of Chicago, in New York City, in Army intelligence and propaganda operations during six campaigns in the Mediterranean and European theaters were better informed than the Nazi victims and the Nazis themselves.

And now I wonder whether to add that, although I have been ignorant of all but the broad media-relayed outlines of Israel history until recently, the Israelis themselves, and by all odds the American Jews have been adequately informed of events in the "Holy Land" and Washington, and what is worse, that they do not now realize or admit to themselves the worsening of their conduct as a state, and how it may well deteriorate to an unforgivable degree as the process moves along.

The USA must get its back up. The US Jews have paid a heavy price for their support of Israel - without even realizing it. Israel has restrained seriously the Jews of the USA even while milking them continuously for every means of support.

Bringing in Israel as a State would go far towards remedying this injurious condition. For the Israelis would be forcibly Americanized, controlled by US Jews and the myriad friends of US Jews who have been muted and abused and helpless for 60 years. We must learn and remember that Israeli Jews have no love for US Jews and to a significant degree are prone to social hooliganism. Private violence is rising significantly in Israel.

Poles and Russians, a million of them, are the weapons of the rabid Israeli elite. They supply many henchmen, thugs, envious of all they have missed over the years. The only way to cure them is to make Americans out of them: they will change overnight, and, though you might not want them to marry your daughter, they cannot help but try their best to repeat the remarkable performance of the Jews of 1890-1970.

Important religious groups of Haredi and others are uncooperative with the military, are exempted from service if proven of priestly or religious preoccupation. The End of the World is expected but they need do nothing to prevent it. One study showed 70% of 375 residents who entered the Haredi community "said they felt they were living in the beginning of a Messianic process." They can do the same in America and the United States has had a long experience handling informally and formally the eccentricities of religious cults.

There exist some 150 psychotherapies (sociotherapies) employing different methods of healing individual and social psyches. In fact, though unnumbered, political and intergroup therapies add to the varieties, and much more need development.

The job of governing, one of its most critical tasks, is to bring about consensus on basic conduct and beliefs among its citizens. A surprising amount of consensus-building has been occurring; more is needed, the task is not so difficult, surely not impossible, and any new State such as Canaan would have every incentive under the USA and its own State Constitution to proceed toward this goal – so unimaginable now, if one is to believe the ignorant, the biased, the truculent, the defiant media and extreme groups in charge of the political elites of the concerned units of government.

We repeat what was said earlier about Mental Health. A State, this State and all others, indeed, should engage heavily in sociotherapy; here we mean the pure and applied sciences of bringing their peoples into better mutual understanding and sympathy. A State composed as ours here, of Israel and Palestine, would appear to present almost insuperable problems in this regard, but certainly not so when we think of successes occurring in the methods of therapy.

The quickness and efficacy of the American melding pot of the many States, individually and as a whole, are rare in history. The two million Jews who emigrated to the USA around the turn of the twentieth century assimilated in work, culture and family with breath-taking rapidity, most certainly not disappearing into a total union of peoples, but blending in every imaginable way, such that no one would have cause for complaint should the same process occur with Canaan – as surely it would.

Many thousands of Palestinians in the prisons of Israel will be promptly released, except in some rare cases where the Israel prosecuting authorities can demonstrate that a rule of law governed the case. As soon as possible, the State's attorney would withdraw all charges on the rest. The State legislature will compensate them for time spent in jail, even though there have been 700,000 of them.

The actions can be ordered by incorporating appropriate clauses in the Act of Admission.

Given the American mosaic culture, given a variety of helpful Jews 50% of them reconciled with Palestinians, the Palestinians would become in two generations a leader of Islamic cultural progress. And Canaan would also be among the top two or three American State cultures. And Canaan might become the means of relating the people of today's Palestine and Israel to its adjoining States as a good neighbor.

The atom bomb is useless for the 7 million Israelis except for committing suicide. For there are scores of missiles ready to fire at Israel from several countries. The moment an apparent nuclear missile is sensed from Israel, or strikes somewhere, these weapons-at-ready will be discharged at Israel.

Although Israel "Samson" might devastate neighboring populations with its nuclear bombs, radioactive fallout will cause it great harm.

AIPAC was a centerpiece in the tableau of Jewish lobbies described by Professors Walt and Mersheimer of Harvard and Chicago respectively. They were securely entrenched, could not be fired, but had to endure attacks that would have downed lesser figures. Paul Findley, a long-time Congressman, documented a number of such cases in his book, *They Dare to Speak Out* (1955-1989-2003). He tells of Senator Charles Percy's unexpected defeat in Illinois when he ran for re-election. An ordinary, rather colorless Jewish Democratic Congressman named Simon was put up to run against Percy, the Republican. He had to be guaranteed heavy support to oppose Percy. He got it. One Los Angeles "Israeli-Freak" contributed well over a million "twice-the-present-value"dollars to beat him. Afterwards, Thomas A. Dine, Director of AIPAC, said: "All the Jews of America, from coast to coast, gathered to oust Percy. And American politicians - those who hold positions now and those who aspire - got the message."

My friend and waterpolo teammate in college,'Chuck' Percy was honest, gravely serious, diligent and certainly not antisemitic. He was one of the best of the U.S. Senators. His support for Jewish and Israeli causes was taken for granted. He visited Israel, made mild but significant criticism of

Israeli conduct. That was enough to bring AIPAC and the whole Israel network into action. He lost narrowly. However, re-reading the remark of Dine, above, I may ask Dine to estimate for me how many American politicians, those in office and those waiting to run for office, quit politics, toed the Israeli line, and defied the message (and of these how many succeeded in any event and how many were knocked out).

The world of public policy should have long ago recognized and confessed that there was a second strong side to the Israeli-Palestinian controversy. Persons such as Buber, Gandhi, Arendt, Barenboim, and Carter do not play games here. Daniel Barenboim had crossed swords with the Israeli censors and Zionists some time before, when he had performed music of Richard Wagner.

But let us take up the case of Wagner. Wagner has been reputed to be anti-Semitic, going back for over a century. Suffice to say that Wagner collaborated with Jews and criticized Jews and was criticized by them, and wrote antisemitic panphlets. More important here is his astonishing connection with Israel. In a certain sense, he was the godfather of Israel, for the founder of Zionism, Theodor Herzl, adored Wagner's music and was inspired by it, and claimed that the very idea of an Israeli state came to him while listening to Wagner's opera *Tannhaeuser* - which contains the magnificent chorale of the Pilgrims returning to their homeland.

Like Yahweh, Wagner was always berating his chosen target people. But one could never find a better expression of Yahweh's opinion than Wagner's, who wrote in his diary about the Jews: "When all is said and done, they are still the finest of all" *("...sind sie doch die Allervornehmsten")*.

There is the equally ambiguous case of America's most famous author, Mark Twain, who wrote the best and worst that could be said about Jews. Somehow, not all of this writing is to be found on the Web. It is insightful but exaggerated and unscientific. He passed through Ottoman Palestine, found it desolate and ugly, and therefore is often quoted by those who claim that nothing was there before the Zionists began to move in, drawing with them some Palestinians to whom they afforded a living.

The Israeli government does not provide a generous environment for neighborliness. It may be worth noting that Freemasonry (70 lodges) is one of a very few associations that actively promote better understanding between the different ethnic and cultural segments of Israeli society, particularly between Jewish and Arab brethren.

The Palestinians, quite unlike the native American Indians in regard to Europeans, were and are closely related to the Israeli Jews. They share closely related Semitic languages, always have been and are genetically related to the Jews.

Their Islamic religion is closely related to Israeli Judaism as far back as the mythically claimed father of both Muslims and Jews, Abraham, and many other ancestor. Indeed one could assert and argue that the Israeli-Palestinian conflicts are fratricidal and furthermore, just as many Jews participate in European culture, Palestinians, together with many Jews, share in the great creative civilization of Islam.

Human groups (up to and including civilizations) when struck by sudden, widespread and intensely effective events called by us Quantavolutions, suffer catastrophes and anastrophes, great "destructive" and "constructive" changes.

In the Iron Age, the greater Mediterranean world, if not indeed the whole world, suffered vast natural changes. Many civilizations changed drastically, among them the Greek and the Hebrew.

The Greeks went into a broadened period of pre-socratic philosophy, city-states, scientific movements. Quite differently, the Judaic Hebrews went into a fierce uptight religion. The Greeks climaxed with Aristotle, the Hebrews with Hezekiah. The Greek Quantavolution is continued in modern science, to which many of Hebrew origins, that is, Jews, have joined and made the most brilliant contributions. The Yahwehists traits are still recognizable in the ritualistic, aggressive Torah, in Maimonides, and the Zionists.

Already mentioned were the linguistics and genetic affinities of the two Semitic groups. Other cultural traits are shared. The ritual of circumcision is compulsory in both Islam and Judaism. Greeks and Romans abhorred the practice and promoted the opposite, extended prepuces, as a mark of beauty.

Endeavoring to demean Palestinians, Israeli education suppresses and suffers from ignorance of the great contributions that the Arabs and Muslims have made to culture in times gone by in art, design, literature, music, architecture, philosophy, mathematics and astronomy.

It is worrisome to note and probably a sign of the endemic PTSD affecting Israel society, that the Israel government and allied media around the world are whipping up emotions that many observers believe will end in a preemptive attack by the USA against Iran, on grounds that Iran refuses to admit all that it is doing to create atomic energy and probably ultimately atomic weapons.

Israel has alone of the nations refused to declare whether it has nuclear weapons and enter into arms limitations concerning them, although it has hundreds. Mordecai Vanunu, an Israeli technician who revealed to a British newspaper the extent of Israel's program at Dimona was jailed for 18 years and released after many years only under severe restrictions. He became a Christian and seeks Palestinian citizenship, scorning Israel for its violations of civil rights and great weapons production.

The atmosphere in Israel and America is felt by many to menace liberty of person and expression. History recalls to us that a Senator Joseph Mc Carthy once went on an anti-red binge claiming, to begin with, that the State Department was infested with communists and spies and thereafter extending his investigations and claims to the Army and other departments and public figures, in the period 1951-4, until "condemned" (censored) by the Senate on two insignificant counts out of many. His smear tactics damaged the reputation of many people and organizations. To be called a "red" by Joe McCarthy or his assistants (especially two Jewish lawyers on his staff) hurt and frightened professors, civil servants and public figures. The conservative media were quick to spread McCarthyism. His popularity in Gallup polls never exceeded 50% "favorable" (Jan. 1954). He died at 48 of acute hepatitis (alcoholism), giving his name, "McCarthyism" to the kind of panic-inducing, reckless investigating and red-baiting resembling irresponsible accusations of anti-Semitism for anyone not pro-Israel, especially of the years post-1980, resulting in damaged reputations and silencing of thousands of would-be critics. McCarthyism was reinforced by a House Committee on Un-American Activities that carried on a harrowing circus of misconduct at the same time, spreading panic and paranoia, especially in the arts.

Not only have the Palestinians been deprived of their authorized retaliation, or equal exchange of violence. But also they are outnumbered even when they employ suicide bombers, who on the average kill two Israelis per suicide.

In the gay fierce competition to participate in the killing of the enemy, American factory workers, often women, would inscribe their name or another on a shell or a vehicle, like "Maisie made this!" Every Israeli soldier is equipped with a hundred "Maisies" who designed his equipment and arms, fed him and brought him to where he might kill or injure a Palestinian. That is, if a soldier who fires a projectile is accountable for its effects, so in the chain of weapons designers, planners, manufacturers, shippers, bookkeepers, supply-room personnel, trainers and superior commanders who got him to where he can "blow away" at Palestinians, hopefully armed Palestinians but usually not. It takes a heap of the world's greatest technology and human organization to kill a baby far away. A brother-in-law across the ocean wrote me during the winter of the Battle of Cassino how hard his zipper-factory was working to outfit the Thunderbolt fighters that were in the sky above me: had I seen them? He made a nice sum of money.

So we are dealing on the Palestinian side with a fragmentalized, poverty-stricken (70%), unemployed (70%), arrested and imprisoned (50,000), "ungainfully employed" and incrementally tormented over 60 years, 8 million persons, not to mention many thousands living in other Arab countries, Europe, and the Americas.

Half are cut off from health services by the Wall. 50% suffer from PTSD.

We must conquer religious dread, and we must, Jews must, face the fact that they have given us a harsh god, that the New Testament's forgiving Jesus does not supplant the gods of the Old Testament. We must go beyond Jesus.

The reason is that great gods are born out of quantavolutions, world catastrophes of ancient times. Messiahs such as Jesus and Muhammad must be hooked onto the old great gods whose grip on most people has never been sufficiently relaxed and may be seared into the collective unconscious permanently.

All we can say is that we must somehow learn to despise the punitive gods whose images turn man against man in their name, in the belief of their slightest different characteristics.

The international gay (homosexual) movement was scheduled to meet in Israel recently, but was blocked by rightist parties dominated by religious extremists. When at the same time minor earthquakes shook the Jordan Valley, a member of the Shass party orated on the floor of the Knesset that they were caused by the homosexual plan. His party, with 12 of the 120 seats, agreed.

Its leader, Rabbi Ovadia Yossef, also believes that the vastly destructive New Orleans hurricane "Katrina" was sent by God, because the USA was pressing the Israeli government to dismantle an illegal settlement, Gush Katif.

When you come to think of it, with the exception of some exempted orthodox believers, every healthy young Israeli man (and many women) have had to take their turn at physically beating up, chasing, blocking, threatening, insulting other human beings of all ages and on numerous occasions. This conduct resembles all too poignantly the despicable jew-baiting of Europeans and Americans of all classes over the ages.

Aggressivity in the Israeli population is excessive. I have an Israeli friend who is a a street artist: he is a fire-eater and also freezes into human "marble" statues. Thus he makes his living. His name is Lee. He performs now only in European cities. He has left Israel in dismay at the pervasive spirit of intolerance and violence there: Israeli children used to react aggressively, attack and kick him while he was doing his act. Recent studies have shown increases in violence generally. Universal training in tolerance, sympathy and compassion is much needed in Canaan – and indeed everywhere.

The worse the battle field plight of the German armies and the civil population, the more anxious and derelict became the Germans in charge of the extermination program; the call to destroy the enemies of the Third Reich in the field put upon themselves their duty of executing Jews and the others. Any and all methods were resorted to. The insanity of the last weeks of the war found dutiful death-camp soldiers marching their near-death "charges" along the roads going West to keep them "from falling into the hands of the advancing Russians," they said.

The opposite behavior, one thinks, could just as well have been expected. Seeing utter defeat at hand, the Exterminators might have stopped their job, gotten lax, deserted – and some did so, here and there; but generally they felt damned if they did not carry out, indeed accelerate, their performance of duty. (Just before American soldiers arrived, the Dachau Camp garrison fled, leaving heaps of dead saturated in lime and a skeletal crowd of prisoners.)

The more that Jews (and Israelis) live under the Shoah trauma, the more punitive their behavior toward the Palestinians will tend to be. Unless they are compelled to realize this, they will repeat the worst symptoms of PTSD. This is what Velikovsky implied in his study of *Mankind in Amnesia.* He could not let himself say so explicitly, because he would have suffered keenly, hurt his family's feelings, and lost some of his fundamentalist supporters. He suppressed the truth in print, although he had to admit it in conversations with close friends.

The "Chosen People" would need to turn themselves around, and choose the other path, lest matters degenerate further, for everybody. Again and again, we must repeat: the worse the rogue elite behaves, the worse conditions will likely become for all Israelis and for Jews in general, and by extension, for a wide-spreading band of humanity.

The rogue Israeli elite welcomes thousands of American fundamentalists as tourists. They give forceful political support to Israel in America, as well as bring in needed dollars. It conceals its discouraging of Christian groups that have been there for centuries, and yet would have it no other way. The Christian churches, intimidated like most others by the Shoah, hardly let out murmurs of pain, with an occasional call to boycott the country's corporate suppliers from abroad. The Church, Thank God! - ain't what it used to be.

Withal, I quote these words of the philosopher and early Palestine resident, Martin Buber, who believed, like myself, in a single union of the two peoples. This holy dreamtime should be a "functional federalism," or so I called it:

> "Our settlers do not come here as do the colonists from the Occident to have natives do their work for them; they themselves set their shoulders to the plow and they spend their strength and their blood to make the land fruitful. But it is not only for ourselves that we desire its fertility. The Jewish farmers have begun to teach their brothers, the Arab farmers, to cultivate the land more intensively; we desire to teach them further: together with them we want to cultivate the land - to 'serve' it, as the Hebrew has it. The more fertile this soil becomes, the more space there will be for us and for them. We have no desire to dispossess them: we want to live with them. We do not

want to dominate them: we want to serve with them..."

The voice, the tone, the compassion, the wisdom, the dream. What a tragic contrast to the many years that followed, the whole history of a country, Israel. Near the eve of the 60th Anniversary on May 8, 2008, of its assumption of statehood, Israel's soldiery were mercilessly attacking Gaza. Their pretext was the sporadic crude rockets that fell upon the nearby town of Ashkelon. An Israeli soldier had been killed, the first one since February. Meanwhile many Palestinians had been killed and buildings destroyed. In April, as a retaliation, many more Palestinians were killed and the Hamas Gaza City Center partially destroyed.

The Israel Vice Minister of Defense, Matan Vinai, declared on the occasion: "The more intense the rocket fire from Qassam, the greater the Shoah to which they expose themselves. This is important because we will use all our strength to defend ourselves." 'Shoah' is the correct Hebrew word for 'Holocaust,' meaning literally 'catastrophe.' The term, the world knows, is emotionally loaded, and strikes fear to the human heart everywhere. Those who act it out, and furthermore call it by its name, are beyond the frontiers of sanity.

Extended Sources relative to the Statehood of Canaan

There is a unique story behind the admission to the Union of every American State. The Web (including Wikipedia) gives copious material and linkages in every case. I have merely called attention to events somehow pertinent to the Canaan Case. My own works on American and world politics and history provide background information and theories of "good government."

The awesome Web, I can practically guarantee, will afford a person sources that are related to any clause of this book. What follows here is a short Bibliography of readily available works that expand the argument of the book. (A Google search of the Internet gives 310,000,000 hits to the word "Israel." and 50,900,000 hits to the word "Palestine.") Mentions of additional sources are scattered throughout the text.

Bibliography

Amnesty International for its news and reports regularly. See http://web.amnesty.org
Aturi, Nasser: *Dishonest Broker: The Role of the United States in Palestine and Israel* (South End Press, 2003)

Ben-Yehuda, Nachman: *The Masada Myth: Collective Memory and Mythmaking in Israel (U of Wisconsin,* 1995)

Birnbaum, Philip: *The Torah and the Haftarot* (Heidenheim Hebrew text with English translation by Birnbaum, Hebrew Publ. Co., 1983)

Blum, William: *Rogue State* (Common Courage Press, 2005)

Chomsky, Noam: *The Fateful Triangle* (South End Press, 1999)

Cutler, Irwin, David Matas, and Stanley A. Urman: *Jewish Refugees from Arab Countries* (Justice for Jews from Arab Countries,<http://www.JusticeforJews.com> 2007)

Davis, Uri: *Apartheid Israel* (Zed, 2003)

de Grazia: Alfred, *The Iron Age of Mars,* 2 vols. (Metron, 2007)

de Grazia: Alfred, *Complete Works,* <http://www.grazian-archive.com>. (Also available on DVD)

Drury, Shadia B.: *Leo Strauss and the American Right* (Griffin, 1999)

Encel, Frederic: *Geopolitique de Jerusalem* (Flammarion, 1998)

Findley, Paul: *They Dared to Speak Out: People and Institutions Confront Israel's Lobby* (Lawrence Hill, 2003)

Finkelstein, Norman G.: *The Holocaust Industry* (Verso, 2000)

Finkelstein, Norman G.: *Image and Reality of the Israel-Palestine Conflict* (Verso, 2003)

Finkelstein, Norman G.: *Beyond Chutzpah: On the Misuse of AntiSemitism* (Verso, 2005)

Finkelstein, Israel and Neil Asher Silberman: *The Bible Unearthed* (Touchstone, 2002)

Fox, Edward: *Palestine Twilight: The Murder of Dr. Albert Glock and the Archaeology of the Holy Land* (Harper Collins, 2001)

Gottwald, Norman: *The Tribes of Yahweh* (Maryknoll, 1979)

Guigne, Bruno: *"Quand le lobby pro-Israélien se déchaîne contre l'ONU,"* http://oumma.com/Quand-le-lobby-pro-israelien-se 13 mars 2008

Hedges, Chris: *War is a Force that Gives Us Meaning* (Anchor books, 2003)

Hersh, Seymour: *The Samson Option* (Random House, 1991)

Hilberg, Raul: *The Destruction of the European Jews* (Holmes and Meier, 1985)

Holocaust:
<http://www.cactus48.com/holocaust.html> (*2008*)

Ketzer, Morris N.: *What's a Jew?* (World, 1978)

Khalidi, Rashid: *Palestinian Identity* (Columbia U.,1997)

Koestler, Arthur: *The Thirteenth Tribe: The Khazar Empire and Its Heritage* (Random House, 1976)

Kovel, Joel: *Overcoming Zionism* (Pluto, 2007)

Lasswell, Harold D. and Abraham Kaplan: *Power and Society* (Yale, 1950)

Levene, Mark and Penny Roberts, eds.: *The Massacre in History* (Berghahn Books, 2006)

Lewis, Bernard: *What Went Wrong* (Oxford U. Press, 2002)

Maimonides*: Sefer Hamitzvot (Book of the 613 Mitzvot), 12th Century* Masalha, Nur*: Expulsion of the Palestinians* (Institute Palestine Studies, 1992)

Mearsheimer, John J. and Stephen M. Walt*: The Israel Lobby and U.S. Foreign Policy* (Farrar, Straus, Giroux, 2007)

Morris, Benny*: Righteous Victims* (Vintage, 2001)

Neff, Donald: *"Truman Overrode Strong State Department Warning..."* Washington Report, October 1994

Nitzan, Jonathan and Shimson Bichler*: The Global Political Economy of Israel* (Pluto, 2002)

Pappe, Ilan*: A History of Modern Palestine* (Cambridge U, 2004)

Petras, James*: The Power of Israel in the United States* (Clarity Press, 2006)

Polk, William R.: *Violent Politics* (Harper Collins, 2007)

Qumsiyeh, Mazin B.*: Sharing the Land of Canaan* (Pluto, 2004)

Rampton, Sheldon and John Stauber: *Weapons of Mass Deception: The Uses of Propaganda in Bush's War on Iraq* (Robinson, 2003)

Sachar, M.: *A History of Israel: From the Rise of Zionism to Our Time* (Knopf, 1996)

Said, Edward W.: *Out of Place* (Granta, 2000)

Salibi, Kamal: *The Bible Came from Arabia* (Jonathan Cape, 1985)

Salibi, Kamal: *The Historicity of Biblical Israel* (Nabu, 1998)

Samora, Julian and Simon, Patricia: *A History of the Mexican-American People* (Notre Dame, 1993)

Sand, Shlomo: *Comment le Peuple Juif fut Inventé* (Fayard, 2008) - soon to appear in English translation

Shabtai, Aharon: *J'Accuse* (poetry) (New Directions, 2003)

Shahak, Israel and Norton Nezvinsky: *Jewish Fundamentalism in Israel* (Pluto, 1999)

Shahak, Israel: *Open Secrets: Israeli Nuclear and Foreign Policies* (Pluto, 1997)

Silberman, Charles E.: *A Certain People: American Jews and Their Lives Today* (Summit, 1985)

Siu, R.G.H.: *Panetics Trilogy of Suffering* (3 vols.,International Society for Panetics, 1993)

Tal, Allon: *Pollution in a Promised Land* (UC Berkeley, 2002)

Todd, Emmanuel and Bourbage, Youssef: *Le Rendez-Vous des Civilisations* (Seuil, 2007)

Tilley, Virginia: *The One-State Solution* (U of Michigan, 2005)

Tubb, Jonathan N.: *Canaanites* (U. Oklahoma, 1999)

United Nations Commission on Human Rights: See its indexed reports.

United Nations General Assembly and Security Council: Search Resolutions for indexed relevant votes

United States, the Central Intelligence Agency maintains updated on-line statistical handbooks of Israel and Palestine.

Valebrega, Guido, Ed.: *Palestina e Israele: Un Confronto Lungo un Secolo tra Miti e Storia* (Teti, 1999)

Velikovsky, Immanuel: *Mankind in Amnesia* (Doubleday, 1982)

Works by Alfred de Grazia

Political Science:

Human Relations in Public Administration: an Annotated Bibliography from the Fields of Anthropology, Public Administration Service, Chicago, 1949.

Roberto Michels: First Lectures in Political Sociology, Translation and Introduction, University of Minnesota Press, 1949.

An Outline of International Relations, (with George B. de Huszar), Barnes & Noble, New York, 1951.

Public and Republic: Political Representation in America, Alfred A. Knopf, New York, 1951, 1953; Greenwood Press, Westport, Conn., 1985.

The Elements of Political Science: vol. 1: *Political Behavior;* vol. 2: *Political Organization,* Alfred A. Knopf, New York, 1952.

The Western Public, Stanford University Press, 1954.

The American Way of Government, Wiley, New York, 1957.

Grass Roots Private Welfare, editor, New York University Press, 1958. *American Welfare,* with Ted Gurr, New York University Press, 1961.

World Politics: A Study in International Relations, (with Thomas H. Stevenson), Barnes & Noble, New York, 1962, 1966.

Politics and Government: the Elements of Political Science, Collier Books, New York, 1962.

Essay on Apportionment and Representative Government, American Enterprise Institute for Public Policy Research, Washington, 1963.

Apportionment and Representative Government, Praeger, New York, 1963; Greenwood Press, Westport, Conn., 1983.

Revolution in Teaching: New Theory, Technology, and Curricula, editor, (with David A. Sohn), Bantam Books, 1964.

Programs, Teachers and Machines, editor, (with David A. Sohn), Bantam Books, 1964.

Republic in Crisis: Congress Against the Executive Force, Federal Legal Publications, New York, 1965.

International Affairs: an annotated and intensively indexed compilation of significant books, pamphlets and articles..., (w. Carl E. Martinson and John B. Simeone), Universal Reference System, general editor, New York, 1965.

Twelve Studies of the Organization of Congress, coordinator, American Enterprise Institute for Public Policy Research, Washington, 1966.

Congress, The First Branch of Government, editor, Doubleday-Anchor Books, 1967.

Congress and the Presidency: Their Roles in Modern Times, with Arthur M. Schlesinger, American Enterprise Institute for Public Policy Research, Washington, 1967.

Bibliography of Bibliographies in Political Science, Government, and Public Policy..., general editor, Universal Reference System, Princeton Research Publications, 1968.

The Behavioral Sciences: Essays in honor of George A. Lundberg, editor, Behavioral Research Council, Great Barrington, Mass., 1968.

Public Opinion, Mass Behavior, and Political Psychology..., (w. Carl E. Martinson and John B. Simeone), Universal Reference System, creator and general editor, Princeton Research Publications, 1969.

Economic Regulation: Business and Government..., general editor, (w. Carl E. Martinson and John B. Simeone), Universal Reference System, Princeton Research Publications, 1969.

Public Policy and the Management of Science..., general editor, (w. Carl E. Martinson and John B. Simeone), Universal Reference System, Princeton Research Publications, 1969.

Administrative Management: Public and Private Bureaucracy..., general editor, (w. Carl E. Martinson and John B. Simeone), Universal reference System, Princeton Research Publications, 1969.

Comparative Government and Cultures..., general editor, (w. Carl E. Martinson and John B. Simeone), Universal Reference System, Princeton Research Publications, 1969.

Current Events and Problems of Modern Society..., (w. Carl E. Martinson and John B. Simeone), Universal Reference System, Princeton Research Publications, 1969.

Kalos: What is to be done with our World? Popular Prakashan, Bombay, 1970.

Old Government, New People: Readings for the New politics, et al., Scott, Foresman, Glenview, Ill., 1971.

Politics for Better or Worse, Scott, Foresman, Glenview, Ill., 1973.

Eight Branches of Government: American Government Today, w. Eric Weise, Collegiate Pub., 1975.

Eight Bads - Eight Goods: The American Contradictions, Doubleday Anchor Books, 1975.

Supporting Art and Culture: 1001 Questions on Policy, Lieber-Atherton, New York, 1979.

A Cloud Over Bhopal: Causes, Consequences, and Constructive Solutions, Kalos Foundation for the India-

America Committee for the Bhopal Victims: Popular Prakashan, Bombay, 1985.

Quantavolution

The Velikovsky Affair: The Warfare of Science and Scientism, University Books, New Hyde Park, NY, 1966. Sphere Books, London, 1978.

Chaos and Creation: an Introduction to Quantavolution in Human and Natural History, Metron Publications, 1981.

The Divine Succession: a Science of Gods Old and New, Metron Publications, 1983. 2nd edition : 2015

Homo Schizo, 2 v., Metron Publications, 1983. 2nd edition: 2014-2015

God's Fire: Moses and the Management of Exodus, Metron publications, 1983. 2nd edition : 2013

The Lately Tortured Earth: Exoterrestrial Forces and Quantavolution in the Earth Sciences, Metron Publications, 1983. 2nd edition : 2016

The Disastrous Love Affair of Moon and Mars: Celestial Sex, Earthly Destruction, and Dramatic Sublimation in Homer's Odyssey, Metron Publications, 1984.

The Burning of Troy and Other works in Quantavolution and Scientific Catastrophism, Metron Publications, 1984.

Cosmic Heretics: A Personal History of Attempts to establish and Resist Theories of Quantavolution... 1963-1983, Metron Publications, 1984. 2nd edition : 2013

Solaria Binaria: Origins and History of the Solar System, w. Prof. Earl R. Milton, Metron Publications, 1984.

The Iron Age of Mars, Metron Publications, 2009

Autobiography & Poetry

Passage of the Year, poetry, Quiddity Press, Princeton, 1967.

The Student: At Chicago in Hutchins' Hey-Days, Quiddity Press, Princeton, 1991.

The Fall of Spydom: Memoir of a Case of Espionage..., Quiddity Press, Princeton, 1992.

The Babe: Child of Boom and Bust in Old Chicago, Umbilicus Mundi, Quiddity Press, Princeton, 1992.

A Taste of War: Soldiering in World War II., Metron Publications, Princeton, 2011.

Twentieth Century Fire Sale, poetry, Quiddity press, Princeton, 1996.

Published on the Web only

Letters of Love and War (1942-1945), war-front and home-front correspondence with Jill Oppenheim de Grazia <http://www.grazian-archive.com/love_letters_NEW/>1997

Plays,<http://www.grazian-rchive.com/poetry/plays/contents/>, 1997.

Almost all the works of the author can be consulted on his website:

<http://www.grazian-archive.com>